MASTER
EXCELLENCE

13 Principles to Help You Win at Life

Adeyinka Adegbenle

Master Excellence
13 Principles to Help You Win at Life

ISBNs:
978-1-7362207-3-3 (hardcover)
978-1-7362207-4-0 (paperback)

Published by:
Ways of Excellence
www.yinkaadegbenle.com

To everyone who gets up daily and gives their best, even in the midst of personal issues you may be facing, thank you! You challenge us to be better, and the world is a better place because of people like you. We need more individuals like you on this planet.

CONTENTS

INTRODUCTION

Why Excellence?

WHAT DOES IT MEAN to live a life of excellence? For me, it means living your life to make an impact and a difference while you are here on this planet. You do not need a huge platform to make a difference. You can make a conscious decision to make a positive difference where you are right now. If you are a parent, excellence is making up your mind to be the best parent you can possibly be to your children. If you are a teacher, excellence is making the commitment to leave an indelible mark on the students that you teach by choosing to be the best teacher you could possibly be every time you interact with your students.

Excellence does not happen accidentally. It is intentional and requires making a conscious decision to operate at a higher level. A person of excellence operates with the right intentions, but not because they are expecting an accolade or reward—far from it. A person of excellence is internally motivated to go the extra mile and give their best because they know that it is the right thing to do. They get a deep sense of satisfaction from doing and giving their best. Anything less than that would be considered unacceptable.

Practicing excellence comes down to striving for the highest possible standards in one's life by committing to doing the best with the available resources one has now. The practice and pursuit of excellence involves motion—taking action with what you have now. It means not waiting for circumstances to align perfectly, but instead learning to work with what is available to you now. More may become available in the future, but it also may not. A person of excellence is not going to wait to find out. They will take action with the resources at their disposal now and utilize those resources to the best of their ability. When more does eventually come into their life—increased income, a new opportunity—they will be ready to make the most of it.

Motion leads to the discovery of strengths and abilities we probably did not even realize that we had in the first place. By taking the best option available to us toward the achievement of a set goal or dream, we discover great things about ourselves that we would not have otherwise uncovered, had we chosen to remain stagnant or not made a move out of fear and the many "but what ifs?" in life. We would also have never gotten to experience the gratification of personal growth as a result.

Let me consolidate what I've said above into a succinct definition of excellence: Excellence is doing your best with what you have now while developing the capacity to handle more.

It is a well-known fact that we plant today the harvest of tomorrow. The truth about living a life of excellence is this: our actions are like seeds, and we do eventually reap what we sow. The things we do now will determine what we will experience later in life. Actions come with consequences, and those consequences can impact our future negatively or positively. Choosing to live

2

a life of excellence is choosing to sow good seeds toward one's future. Just as a person who exercises regularly and consistently eats a healthy diet will over time reap a harvest of good health and agility, a person who purposefully chooses to live a life of excellence will reap a bountiful harvest of the many great benefits a life of excellence has to offer.

Excellence pays great dividends now and in the future. It has many advantages. The different stories and examples scattered throughout this book of various clients I have worked with over the years showcase the many great benefits of living a life of excellence. Reflecting on the work I've done with clients, I can attest that a few of those benefits are that you will grow and mature intellectually, and that you will also experience a satisfying and fulfilling life. Another major advantage of choosing excellence is this: You will most definitely learn how to present yourself to the world in a positive way. You will master tact and much more by the time you get to the end of this book. Choosing to operate in excellence in the workplace will distinguish you from most of your coworkers, because sooner than later the decision-makers at your place of work will take notice, and that could lead to a promotion and more.

Choosing to live a life of excellence has other tremendous benefits, both for yourself and those closest to you. By choosing excellence, you are indirectly choosing to build a legacy that will far outlive you. When your children see and emulate your excellent choices, they will also in turn pass those same values down to their children, and their children will do the same.

There are so many people living life well below what they are truly capable of. Their true potential lies dormant because they have settled into a place of comfort. But deep down they feel a gnawing sense of discomfort because they know that they are capable of doing more with their lives. But they lack the understanding of how and where to begin to take that journey of discovery toward living a full life, a life that far surpasses mediocrity. A life that does not make them feel as though they are stuck and just going through the motions or, worse still, living their life in cruise control mode. They do not know how to achieve a satisfying life that would allow them to operate at their highest level.

We fear that we may get to the end of life and discover that we could have done so much more because we were capable of so much more. But we let a lack of understanding on how to do "the so much more" hold us back and keep us locked in a place of mediocrity. If this resonates with you, then you are most certainly in the right place. I have written this book to serve as the blueprint, the manual that you need to help you move from living your life, day in and day out, on cruise control and move *toward* actually seizing the horns and becoming everything you were created to be.

I will show you how to live a full life through the thirteen principles of excellence presented in this book. These principles will help you to discover your potential and unlock the door to your future. Where you have once felt you were lacking, you will discover that you actually have all that you need at your disposal to become the best version of yourself.

You will get to discover that your abilities and capabilities are not fixed, but are waiting for you to help them grow and evolve. You will see that you are capable of so much more. As you step out and put into practice the different excellence principles in this book, you will gradually start to evolve into a person of excellence—a masterpiece uniquely created with a purpose and great capabilities. You will find fulfillment and arrive at a place of peace.

No longer will you live "less than." Your horizons will broaden, and you will take charge of your life, approaching it with courage, confidence, and enthusiasm.

You will realize that the only way to become your highest possible self is through living in excellence, and that will inevitably impact your approach to life, mindset, the standards that you hold (you will end up developing an intolerance for mediocrity, laziness, and excuses), and everything else you do and say to yourself to remain comfortable but deeply unfulfilled.

You will also come to realize that you are not in competition with anyone else but yourself. You have been created with purpose to run your own life's race and to run it well. Not to compare your life with another or compete with another. As a matter of fact, your only "competition" will be a fulfilling, never-ending journey toward becoming a better, improved version of who you were yesterday or the month before.

My Journey to Excellence

I did not just wake up one day and decided to become a person with a deep affinity for excellence, its practices, and its pursuits. I coasted and cruised through life for quite some time until life happened to me and I was jolted out of my deep and comfortable sleep of mediocrity. My quest for excellence started over a decade ago.

It has been fifteen-plus years and I still remember vividly being called into my manager's office one afternoon in March in 2009. With a straight, stoic face, she told me that my position had just been eliminated due to the major economic downturn and decline in business.

It was not as though I did not know that this could be an eventual possibility. This was smack in the middle of the Great Recession of 2009. I had watched as several other colleagues had been let go. Still, my layoff came as a shock. I was not sure which made it worse: the fact that I was very unprepared for this job loss financially or that somehow I wrongly assumed I was immune to the impact of the economic downturn, even though it had already profoundly affected the organization where I worked at the time.

When I lost my job, I was heavily pregnant with my second child and in my third trimester. My husband and I had also just purchased our home in the suburbs of Long Island, NY. Our fast-growing family facilitated that decision. I made a pretty good salary and just somehow naively assumed I would always have a job at the Fortune 500 corporation where I worked.

Now overnight, my family went from a two-income family to a one-income family. We were just starting to adapt to paying a monthly mortgage and all else that comes with owning a home.

As the weeks passed, my initial sense of deep shock and panic slowly morphed into sadness and hopelessness. Then it got worse: I blamed myself for the difficult financial position I had put my family in. I imagined worst-case scenarios like losing our newly purchased home, not being able to care for the baby, and more. In addition to these heightened emotions were the elevated hormonal changes that accompany pregnancy. I was a mess!

Thankfully, none of the worst-case scenarios I imagined came to pass, but it was during that time of struggle that I started to deeply reflect on my life. I made the decision to do better . . . in *all* areas. This led me on a path of personal development. I was hungry and determined to learn everything learnable about how to become a better version of myself, from top to bottom.

It was while on this personal development journey that I discovered what I now call The 13 Excellence Principles. Every time I succinctly identified one of these Excellence Principles, it felt as though I had somehow accidentally discovered gold!

In this book I have documented each one of these thirteen principles. I have tested them time and time again, first on myself, and then on the many clients I have worked with in my Excellence Development Coaching Program over the years. The many small business owners and clients who I have worked with can attest to the positive results of applying these principles to their lives. Their results have been unbelievable!

These principles are universal! They work irrespective of the part of the world you live in, your age, or your demographics and socioeconomic status. These principles *will* work for you, and will produce results that will elevate your life to new heights.

What to Expect from Each Chapter

In each chapter, an Excellence Principle is explained, followed by case studies and practical examples. The Points to Remember at the end of each chapter will help to solidify all you have learned in the chapter and also serve as a source of reflection.

To get the most out of this book, be sure to do the work outlined in each chapter's Take Action section. As you read each chapter, underline or highlight meaningful passages for later reference, and then start to think of ways to apply the principles to your own personal life and circumstances.

After all, knowledge without application is simply that— knowledge. Knowledge has to be put into practice for you to gain its full benefits. By the end of this book, I know that you will be driven to relentlessly pursue and master excellence in every area of your life.

CHAPTER 1

WHAT IS EXCELLENCE?

EXCELLENCE IS OPTIMIZING THE resources at our disposal now. It is making the most of the gift of the one life that we have. There is no do over. This is not a dress rehearsal. It is our responsibility to make this one life that we have been gifted with count.

When you pursue excellence in how you live your life, you are choosing to live your life with intentionality. You are choosing to make a positive difference. You are choosing to leave your mark.

When you optimize, you are choosing to do your best with the current resources at your disposal. This allows you to enlarge your capacity for growth, and to make room for bigger and better versions of what you already have to flow into your life. You also increase your level of efficiency while doing so.

After all, why should anyone entrust you with more when you have not successfully proven that you can handle or manage what you have now? That is like handing the keys to a $320,000 Mercedes to a newly licensed 16-year-old who has yet to prove and show that he is a diligent driver. Just because he passed his driving test does not automatically mean his parents would hand him the keys to such an expensive vehicle, even if they could comfortably afford to do so. The wise thing to do is to let him practice and perfect his driving skills in a far less expensive vehicle—a used vehicle, perhaps. When he shows responsibility and proves that he is capable of handling a more expensive car, then he can be handed the keys to the expensive Mercedes, should his parents choose to do so.

Excellence is a mindset. It is a way of life. We are creatures of habit. Usually how we do one thing is how we do everything. So by adopting and developing a mindset of excellence, over time we discover that the mindset of excellence will come to permeate every area of our lives.

It is when we are faithful and good stewards of what we have—such as our finances, gifts, and talents—that we show that we are ready for more. "More" can take many forms. It can be holding a deeper appreciation for what we have now. When we thought we had nothing, or not enough, we now realize how immensely blessed we truly are or have been all along. "More" could be discovering new ways to stretch our current finances further or finding even more uses for our gifts and talents. "More" could also very well be getting a new job with double the salary. By the way, a greater income may mean more responsibilities, but it does not necessarily mean more stress. If you are a business owner, "more" could mean a new contract, more clients, and so on.

We all have been endowed with a special gift or talent. A person with an excellence mindset will discover what that gift is, develop it, hone it, and use it well. Most of us, in fact, have been endowed with *many* gifts and talents. Discovering what those gifts and talents are is one of the major keys to finding fulfillment and contentment in life. More on this later on.

Many times we see others who have discovered, developed, and are now walking and thriving in their areas of gifting. We start to think deprecating thoughts, such as "I was born unlucky" or "I was dealt a bad hand at birth." When truthfully we simply have not taken the time to intentionally discover what our gifting is and then start to walk in that gifting.

Once we discover a gift of ours and we start to walk in it, we then often discover other gifts in the process. Make the most of your current circumstances. Make the most of every opportunity. Don't wait until change comes before you decide to show up as your best self in how you live out your life daily. What if the circumstances do not change, or remain the same for a long time? Excellence is simply being your best now irrespective of your situation or circumstances. It differs for every individual because we are all different and have been dealt different hands in life. Recognize and accept the hand you have been dealt in life and make the most of it. Let me tell you a story that really breaks this down:

Excellence in Practice

I enjoy baking. As a matter of fact, I owned a baking business called Banana Bread to Gò! A few years ago. I made all kinds of delicious banana bread loaves: chocolate chip banana bread, pecan banana bread, toasted walnut banana bread, orange cranberry banana bread . . . you name it. Baking banana bread loaves started off as a hobby and morphed into a business shortly after the birth of my last child. Technically, I was supposed to be taking some time off to care for the baby, but I quickly realized that caring for a newborn left me with ample time to play with, especially after the first few months when the baby had developed a pattern of eating, sleeping, playing, and then sleeping some more.

I knew that it would be hard for me to just sit around doing nothing while the baby slept. Yes, there were other things to do around the house, but I will be the first to admit that I'm a workhorse of sorts.

It was at this point that Banana Bread to Go! was born and, oh, did I have fun baking and selling my loaves. I decided very early on in the business that I would bake the way I eat. I am very particular about ingredients. That translated into using nothing but premium ingredients. This attitude is okay when you are baking for yourself and a few friends. But on a commercial scale, premium ingredients can translate into very pricey very quickly.

I already knew too much about excellence, and was too far gone in my pursuit of excellence in every area, including work, to even try to cut corners in any way. That would be unethical, and there would be no way that I could sleep easy at night, knowing that I did not offer my patrons the very best. But I still had to figure out how to make a profit from this business baking with premium ingredients.

I searched the internet high and low. AI was not a thing back then, so I did my research the old fashioned way via Google, reading through blogs and watching videos. I was determined, and my will and determination eventually paid off. I did quite a bit of testing, and I ended up purchasing a lot of my ingredients—flour, chocolate chips, raisins, you name it—from Trader Joe's. The aforementioned ingredients stocked by Trader Joe's were of superb quality. Butter, sugar, nuts, and other ingredients were purchased from Costco. I was happy to find high quality ingredients that met my standards and with good price points at both stores. I learned to make my own top-quality vanilla extract because I just was not satisfied with the quality of what I purchased elsewhere.

I baked with love and passion. Baking on a large scale is not an easy feat in any way. I have a great deal of admiration for bakers who produce quality baked goods. Believe me, whatever price they charge is well-earned. Baking quality goods with quality ingredients is a labor of love!

I sold my loaves online and at many different fairs on Long Island, NY, in the spring and fall months, mostly. This is not an exaggeration: I sold out almost every single time. I also had several loyal local customers who ordered weekly and came to the different fairs where I sold my baked goods. So I stayed busy baking every week for about four years.

My baking business grew—well, more like exploded. I caught the attention of a popular bakery located in Manhattan. They had somehow tried my baked goods and wanted me to supply them with banana bread loaves. This popular bakery has several stores in Manhattan and is renowned for its delicious quality baked treats.

At that point, I knew that opening a bakery was the next step because I had reached maximum capacity where I was currently. I knew firsthand the type of commitment running the operations of a bakery would entail. I could not wrap my mind around being away from home for sixteen to eighteen hours every day. At this point, I was also starting to feel a strong pull away from baking.

After much deliberation, praying, and introspection, I concluded that opening and running a bakery was not in the works at that point. Plus, I felt strongly compelled to take and share all of the lessons and principles of excellence learned from running my baking business and beyond to the world.

Now, eight years later, I've found my true calling, which is to help others learn about, and grow in, excellence. I do this mainly through my coaching programs, the Master Excellence Course on Teachable, as well as through hosting workshops and seminars on principles, processes, and systems of excellence. Many of the principles came to me while running my baking business.

Ways of Excellence

Ways of Excellence, the parent company of my Excellence Coaching and Consulting business, would probably not have been born if I did not master excellence while running my baking business.

In other words, excellence is mastered in the trenches.

The "more" that we desire, which varies for each individual, will only come about when we are intentional about doing the very best with what we currently have, meaning our current circumstances and the hand that we have been dealt in life. A mindset of excellence realizes that "This is where I am right now, so let me figure out how to make the most of it."

Let me share a couple of additional examples of excellence in action. Let us assume that you suddenly lost your job. Well, it is perfectly understandable to take some time to grieve this loss. You may decide to take a week or a bit longer to do so, and to regroup. But at some point, you will eventually need to replace the lost income with a new one in order to cover your living expenses.

A person of excellence would calibrate and strategize by asking questions such as:

"This is my current situation, how can I make the most of it?"

"This layoff was unexpected. What good can come out of this season of my life?"

"What were the lessons learned from my old job that I need to document and apply to my life now so as to become a better, more valuable employee to my future employer?"

Intentionally choosing to think this way will significantly alleviate the stress from your job loss because the mere act of purposeful thought comforts and reassures the mind. Choosing to stay positive and hopeful will prevent you from spiraling into deep depression. I believe that our subconscious is able to work more efficiently on our behalf when we choose to deliberately redirect our thoughts toward that which is good and solution-oriented. We move in the direction of our thoughts and what we focus on becomes magnified over time. So intentionally choosing to fix our thoughts on what is true, and honorable, and right, and pure, and lovely, and admirable, and excellent is always a good idea and great advice.

Other lines of thought may include:

"Well, I have some free time now. What are the projects that I have put on the back burner for months on end that I can start to work on now as I search for a new job?"

"This may be a great time to start that side hustle that I have had on my vision board for four years in a row."

"I can use this transition period to study for that certification that will add value to me and even help to increase my earning power as an employee in the near future."

In the above examples, there is motion involved. This person is exploring the different ways to make the best use of the interim time before starting a new role. This deliberation and exploration should not take forever. A person of excellence will take the next best option available to them. It could be looking for a part-time job or working in another industry temporarily to cover living expenses as they continue to search for a new long-term role. Or, if they have enough saved financially, preparation toward the certification that will increase their value and worth in the marketplace may be the best option.

Evaluate the circumstances and decide. But do not stay stuck. Get into motion. Do something. This is the type of mindset required to move to the next level and to attract bigger and better things into one's life.

It is acknowledging that yes, you have lost your job, but instead of just focusing on what is not working and how unfair the situation is, an excellence-minded person looks for ways to make the most of what may seem like a dire situation to others.

Excellence-minded people have learned to adopt an eagle-eyed perspective on life's issues. They have a sharp focus on their goals. They are always considering what the next best step to take is, and they are aware that there may be several ways to achieve their short-term and long-term goals. As a result, they remain flexible, open to trying new things. Most times they do not have all of the answers. But they know that the answers will come from taking the next best option and step available to them at any given time. They realize that knowing comes from doing. In life, answers and solutions never appear when we choose to stay stuck.

Your perception on life matters greatly.

Continuing with the job-loss scenario above, another way of shifting the focus away from the negative aspect of the current circumstances is to give thanks for being able to work in your previous organization for however long you worked there. You can show gratitude for the skills learned, for your exposure to new people and new ideas, for how your overall horizons were broadened, for how you grew as a person, and for how you developed as a leader. You can be grateful for the relationships you formed while you were there. For how those people impacted your life. For the lessons gained which you will apply to your new goals and which will help you to evolve and become a better version of yourself. This is the approach of excellence-minded individuals toward life.

Another example: You want a new car. You have been saving up toward getting a new one for sometime now. But, how have you been taking care of the old vehicle that you drive now? Do you consider and treat it like a jalopy that should be in the junkyard as you save toward the new vehicle? Does it look like a dumpster on the inside because you do not even bother taking care of it at all? After all, you are getting a new car someday soon.

This is not about running to the car wash every week. It is more about developing a mindset of being content with what you have now and taking care of it as you await and work toward something better. It is about doing your best with your current circumstances. This in essence is what excellence is and how it works.

Talent and Gifts Are Not Enough

A lot of small businesses start from inside the house. In fact, many hairdressers and bakers run thriving businesses from the confines of their homes. I have come across many highly gifted and talented individuals in my lifetime. However, I've learned that your talents and gifts will only take you so far. Talents and gifts do not necessarily equate to success. Operating in excellence is required!

One of the reasons Banana Bread to Go! grew and thrived was because, even in the early days when I sold mainly from my home kitchen, I made it a point to ensure that cleanliness was a priority. I baked out of a much smaller kitchen than I have now. But I always ensured that the preparation area and the kitchen were clean.

Just the same way you would never eat or buy food from a filthy looking establishment, the customers would not have returned or even told their friends about my baking business if they walked into a filthy space when they came to pick up their orders, or, even worse, a mouse or roach crawled across their feet while they were there.

Yes, Rome was not built in a day. No one expects you to start a business and turn it into an empire overnight. However, while building that catering business or hair salon from your home, make the most of what you have now. Here are a few pointers to assist you:

> The space should be clean and clutter free. This should be nonnegotiable. Your customers deserve to come into a space where they feel comfortable and want to return to because they see the effort you put into ensuring the environment where you work is inviting, clean, and clutter free.

> Even if you happen to be the best and most talented baker or hairdresser in town, if you work out of a filthy space and make no effort to clean and make the space presentable and inviting, most customers will not return. They will go look for another hairdresser who may not be as talented but works out of a clean, clutter-free, inviting space.

People want to patronize your business, but they also want to feel comfortable and safe.

A lot of times, the answer to increasing your customer base is simply taking care of the basics. Skill and talent are just not enough.

How is your character? Are you nice and polite to customers? Or do you berate them and treat them as though they are a bother? Are you condescending or even passive-aggressive toward your customers?

Are you hospitable? Do you have a way of incentivising customers so they come back again and again? (I used to throw in one or two mini-loaves with large banana bread orders.)

Do you go the extra mile to appreciate your customers?

Do you make booking an appointment with you easy? Or do potential customers have to jump through hoops just to get an appointment?

These are just a few things to consider when running your business.

I once met a lady who owned and started a food snack business from her home kitchen. We hit it off when she found out that I also baked from home back then. She asked me to meet her at her house to try samples of her snacks. When I drove up to the house, I was surprised to see how unkempt the front of the house was. She met me by the front door and from where I stood, I was able to see parts of the kitchen and other parts of the house. It was a mess! Sadly, I did not want to risk having food poisoning, based on what I saw. I thanked her for the snacks and took them with me but never tried them because I did not trust the conditions in which they were made. I also could not recommend her business to others in good faith. Unsurprisingly, she did not go very far with her business, and shut it down after only a few months. She was a talented baker, but excellence was lacking because she failed to attend to the basics.

All of what I have talked about can be summarized in this:

"Whoever can be trusted with very little can also be trusted with a lot." —Luke 16:10

To whom much is given, much is expected.

If you cannot be trusted to keep the small vicinity of your home-based business clean, tidy, and inviting, how would you be able to manage a store front? If it is food you are selling, the lack of cleanliness will eventually lead to you having a vermin situation. One direct health code violation and the business will sooner than later shut down.

Master excellence now, in the trenches, as a small business owner so that you can easily excel as a large business owner.

Now that we have covered the underlying thesis of what excellence entails, journey with me as I delve deeper into the Excellence Principles. Be sure you have your pen handy. As I mentioned previously, the last section of each chapter will give you the opportunity to strategize how to apply each of these Excellence Principles to your own life.

KEY POINTS

◎ Excellence is optimizing the resources at your disposal and making the most of your life, irrespective of the hand that you have been dealt.

◎ When you optimize the current resources at your disposal, you enlarge your capacity for more and increase your level of efficiency.

◎ We all have been endowed with at least one special gift or talent. Find out what yours is, develop it, and start to use it. This is one of the keys to finding fulfillment and contentment in life.

◎ It is when we are faithful and good stewards of what we have, including our finances, gifts, and talents, that we show that we are ready for more.

◎ Evaluate your circumstances and decide. But do not stay stuck. Get into motion. Do something. This is the type of mindset required to move to the next level and to attract bigger and better things into one's life.

◎ We are creatures of habit. How we do one thing is usually how we do everything else.

◎ Your perception on life matters greatly. Excellence-minded people have an elevated eagle perspective on life's issues.

◎ Your talents and gifts will only take you so far in life. Talents and gifts do not necessarily equate to success. Excellence is required!

◎ To whom much is given, much is expected.

◎ Master excellence now, in the trenches, as a small business owner so that you can easily excel as a large business owner.

TAKE ACTION

Take some time to reflect on the different areas of your life. Reflection is the process of thinking deeply about something, often with the goal of gaining a better understanding of it. Self-reflection is a required skill for personal growth and the development of excellence in one's life. When we reflect on the different areas of our lives, we are able to evaluate our strengths and weaknesses, identify areas for growth and improvement, and develop strategies that will help us to achieve excellence in those areas.

The different areas to reflect on may include but not be limited to:

◎ health
◎ finances
◎ career
◎ relationships (friendships, extended family)
◎ marriage (if applicable)
◎ spirituality
◎ personal development
◎ mental health

Ask yourself truthfully which areas or categories need improvement the most.

Start from there. Develop an action plan. Take baby steps. It may take you a while to develop a comprehensive plan because you have to do some research and think through your approach over the course of a couple of days. You may even need to solicit the help of a coach. After getting all of the help you need, come up with a plan on how to pursue and grow in excellence in those areas and follow through. Take action, follow your plan, and consistently do what is required to grow in excellence in the areas you have highlighted.

CHAPTER 2

EXCELLENCE PRINCIPLE 1:
Develop Great Daily Routines

WHEN YOU WAKE UP in the morning, what is the first thing you do? Then what do you do next? And then after that? And then after that? You may or may not realize it, but those series of actions that you follow in a sequential manner are called routines.

Routines differ from habits. And routines are a key component of achieving and maintaining excellence.

Habits are actions a person does automatically daily. For example, using the bathroom immediately after waking up in the morning; going to the gym at the same time each day; or brushing your teeth immediately after getting out of bed.

A routine differs from a daily habit in that it is a *series* of actions carried out in sequence to bring order and flow to the day. A great example of a nightly pre-bedtime routine is:

1. Making a to-do list for the next day.
2. Picking out clothes to wear for the next day.
3. Preparing the next day's lunch.
4. Clearing out the sink.

The payoff for this nighttime routine is that it allows you to start each day primed to dive right into your main goals, instead of dealing with a list of small tasks. A well-thought-out routine will help to ensure that a person is making the most of the 24 hours that we all get daily.

A collaborative study led by University of Albany psychologist Jennifer Weil Malatras found that individuals who grow up with predictable, daily routines are less likely to have time-management or attention problems as adults.[1] The study also revealed that consistent mealtimes, among other daily routines, can help children develop good time-management and attention skills.

How Routines Produce Excellence

I have worked with many clients in my one-on-one coaching program. One thing I have discovered is that when a person has an established daily routine, they are more productive and efficient in how they live their lives. In fact, I do not believe it is possible to live a life of excellence without having an established daily routine. Routines are integral to excellence, which is why they are one of the first principles we unpack and work on in my coaching program. Read on to find out why routines are necessary to the development of excellence.

Taking Charge of Your Day

One of the biggest advantages of having routines is being able to take charge and manage one's day. Great time management is imperative to the pursuit of excellence in life. We only have but so many hours each day. It is our responsibility to manage and properly utilize that finite number of hours we have daily.

Here is how my client—we'll refer to her as Rosa—took charge of her day by developing a routine that worked for her schedule. Before working with me, Rosa used to wake up at 7:30 a.m. She works from home, so she would roll right out of bed into her computer chair in her bedroom in her pajamas. She felt like she was always playing catch-up because she lived her life in reactive mode. For the most part, there wasn't any planning involved in terms of how her day would unfold.

After a few sessions with me, we together developed a comprehensive routine that meshed well with her schedule:

Night routine:

> Pick out work clothes for the next day. Wear clothes that spark joy (I learned this from organization expert Marie Kondo).

> Prepare or decide on what you are going to have for lunch the next day. This helped Rosa to make healthy meal choices as opposed to eating whatever snack she had lying around the house or ordering food every afternoon.

> Take a shower/bath at night.

> Write down the three important things she had to get done the next day before going to bed. She did this either right before bed or during her one-hour lunch break.

> Head to bed no later than 10 p.m. Her wake-up time changed to 5:30 a.m.

Read or listen to at least two chapters of a book before falling asleep.

Total time of nightly routine: 45 minutes to 1 hour max.

Morning Routine:

Wake up at 5:30 a.m.

Physically get out of bed for her quiet time: Bible study and prayer; affirmations and meditation.

Light physical exercise, because movement is essential to our total well-being. Before this Rosa had never exercised consistently, so we worked on starting out light and then ramping it up once she established the habit of exercising daily.

She then freshened up and changed into her work clothes.

Work starts at 8 a.m., but because of her efficient new routine she is now able to start at 7:30 a.m. She uses twenty to thirty minutes to plan her work day. As a result, she now has better control of her day as opposed to playing catch-up all the time. She now meets all of her deadlines in good time and has time to enjoy a proper lunch.

After a few weeks of following her schedule consistently, Rosa's confidence level increased dramatically. Her boss recognized and complimented her on the improvement in the quality of her work. She now had time for herself, and even took up a new hobby, tennis. In the past, she felt she had no time at all for any extracurricular activities.

Rosa started eating healthier and saved over $450 monthly by eliminating ordering lunch every day due to a lack of time. By the end of our third month of working together, she was a totally different person.

Wearing work-leisure clothes (clothes that feel and act like exercise clothes but look like work clothes) gave her the comfort and confidence she needed to look the part of a mid-senior executive who worked from home.

As you see from Rosa's positive results, when it comes to your day, you want to be proactive and not reactive, even when you have to adapt to a sudden change of plans. Taking control of your day via well-structured routines will leave you feeling like you are in charge. Routines vary for each individual, but the key is to ensure that your morning routine, in particular, helps you to set the tone for your day.

Order and Structure

The human brain has a strong affinity for structure and order, and responds positively when we implement these qualities in our lives. Order and structure help us feel more in control and less stressed. This is because our brains are wired for categorization, which allows us to categorize objects and concepts quickly and efficiently. The brain responds positively when we have order and structure in our lives. The absence of order and structure can often lead to stress and feelings of unmanageability.

The prefrontal cortex is the specific part of the brain that helps us to create order in our lives. It is responsible for critical thinking and higher cognitive abilities such as decision-making, problem-solving, and planning. Implementing a structure to your day can give you a sense of control and improve your focus, organization, and productivity.

Routines do more than create structure. Good routines can promote mental, physical, and emotional health. Conversely, the absence of such routines can often lead to stress and feelings of unmanageability. If you are looking for a way to add structure and order to your life, having solid routines is the way to go.

Goal Achievement

It will be hard to accomplish much without routines. Routines will help you to prioritize the important things, and as a result, enable you to then plan your day in such a way that you get those important things done.

For instance, if you plan on writing a book. You have to plan your day in such a way as to factor writing into it in order to get the writing done—be it writing daily, every other day, or even just twice a week. To make that happen, you need to carve out writing time as you plan your week. The book is not going to write itself, and the truth is we are all very busy. A well-thought-out writing routine will allow you to carve out the required writing time you need to achieve your goal.

Here's an example from my personal life about the power of routines when it comes to achieving a goal. In 2017, I set out to sit for the PMI-PMP certification exam. The Project Management Professional (PMP) is a globally recognized professional certification offered by the Project Management Institute (PMI). Receiving the PMI certification means they acknowledge you as being highly skilled at managing the people, processes, and business priorities of professional projects. The PMP certification is also accredited against the internationally recognized ISO 9001 and ISO/ANSI 17024 standards.

All of that is to say that the process leading up to obtaining the certification is not only very challenging, but requires plenty of hard work and solid preparation.

I was not grounded in my daily routine the first time I sat for the PMI-PMP certification exam. Needless to say, I failed woefully. Not that I did not study for it; I just underestimated how much work was required. I had studied for this difficult and taxing certification exam in a leisurely manner, and I paid the price. My failure meant money down the drain and having to go through the process leading up to taking the exam again. I was not excited about that. But I had no other choice but to retake the exam.

I realized my previous unstructured approach was insufficient to achieve my goal, so the first thing I did was to develop a routine that accommodated the rigorous demands of preparing for this exam.

I had only two months to prepare to retake the exams due to an impending overhaul of the entire examination system at the time. To put this in perspective, it takes a professional six to eight months to study for the exam ordinarily. Most also get extra help in the form of coaching or additional classes from a seasoned professional well versed in the techniques and strategies of the PMI-PMP exam—just to help them prepare due to the complex nature of the examination. It would have cost me even more money and time if I had chosen to wait for the overhaul to be completed before retaking the exam.

After careful deliberation, the routine I put together looked like this:

Wake up at 5 a.m.

Complete SAVERS by 7:30 a.m. (see the Take Action section at the end of the chapter for more on the powerful SAVERS routine).

Complete work and other home/family related activities by 6:30 p.m.

Go to bed by 7 p.m.

Wake up at 1:00 to 1:30 a.m. to study for the PMI-PMP exam.

Finish studying by 5 a.m. and continue with the rest of my day.

It was a rigorous and taxing routine, but it was the only way that I could fit studying in, due to my other equally demanding commitments at the time. Also, it was a sacrifice I was willing to make for the two months that I had to prepare to retake the exam. Did I feel the pressure? Yes, indeed! And almost every day I had to fight off thoughts of failing a second time.

I had the support of my family, which made adhering to this routine doable. My husband was back from work at 6:30 p.m. every day during the two-month period. On most days, I was already in my pajamas ready for bed as he walked into the house from work.

Well, my sleep-deprived nights and hard work paid off because I aced the exam. I achieved an Above Target rating (the highest possible performance rating that one can get in the exam) in four of the five categories. I achieved an On Target grade in the last category only, missing out on the Above Target rating by just two points. That hurt a little, but nevertheless, I passed the PMI-PMP exam with flying colors! I was beyond elated.

This goal would have been impossible to achieve without a solid routine. And this is just one of many major goals that I have accomplished on the strength of using a well-thought-out routine. Thankfully, the others did not involve sleepless nights for two months straight! I don't think I would have achieved any of my goals without a routine.

Health and Well-being

In addition to the above, routines can also help to establish a healthy, sustainable lifestyle that incorporates self-care into each day. Think of something like meditation, a few minutes of quiet alone time in the mornings. This helps to reduce stress and leads to a better mental state.

While routines can be very beneficial for our mental and physical health, there can be some potential downsides to having a routine if it's not properly thought out. For example, routines can become monotonous and boring if they are not varied or changed up from time to time. Additionally, if we become too reliant on our routines, we may struggle to adapt to new situations or changes in our lives. It is important to find a balance between having routines and being flexible. So look to incorporate some variety into your routines, and be open to change. This will help you avoid any potential downsides.

Overall, establishing well-designed, adaptive routines helps one to grow in excellence and get important things done in a timely manner too. The absence of routines can often lead to feeling overwhelmed and helpless. Having to play catch up due to a lack of order and structure will cause one to feel this way. Daily routines are needed for structure and a logical sequence of actions and activities in our lives. They allow us to experience a flow to our day. Perform your routines with intention and purpose so you see them as meaningful practices that add to your well-being.

Remember: Your routines should not be (or become) another set of mundane habits. You have to carefully craft each routine to help you manage your time and make the most of each day.

KEY POINTS

◎   A series of actions that you follow in a sequential manner is called a routine.

◎   A routine differs from a daily habit in that it is a series of actions carried out in sequence.

◎   Daily routines are needed for establishing structure and a logical sequence in our lives, allowing us to experience a flow to our day.

◎   Daily routines can help children develop good time-management and attention skills.

◎   If you are looking for a way to add structure and order to your life, having a solid routine is the way to go.

◎   The brain responds positively when we have order and structure in our lives.

◎   Order and structure help us feel more in control and less stressed.

◎   If you do not take charge of your day by having routines, life will literally just pass you by.

◎   The absence of routines can often lead to stress and feelings of unmanageability.

TAKE ACTION

My work with coaching clients has shown that the people who "ace" their mornings enjoy the best overall results in terms of excellence and goal-achievement. So with that in mind, I recommend that you develop your personal SAVERS routine. SAVERS is an acronym coined by the best-selling author Hal Elrod in his book *The Miracle Morning*. It stands for: silence, affirmations, visualization, exercise, reading, and scribing.

SAVERS is a six-step morning routine that can help you start your day off on the right foot. The six steps are:

1. Silence: Take a few minutes to meditate, pray, or simply sit in silence.
2. Affirmations: Repeat positive affirmations to yourself to help you stay motivated and focused throughout the day.
3. Visualization: Visualize your goals and aspirations as if they have already been achieved.
4. Exercise: Engage in some form of physical activity to get your blood flowing and boost your energy levels.
5. Reading: Spend some time reading a book or article that inspires you and helps you grow.
6. Scribing: Write down your thoughts, goals, and ideas in a journal or notebook.

A lot of people complete their SAVERS in an hour or two. Design your morning routine to fit your own schedule. Here are some steps to follow:

1. Start small: Begin by incorporating one or two of the SAVERS steps into your morning routine. Gradually add more over time.
2. Be consistent: Make sure to practice the routine every day.
3. Set reminders: Use reminders to help you remember to practice the routine each morning.
4. Track your progress: Keep track of your progress and celebrate your successes along the way.

I suggest reading *The Miracle Morning* to help you develop your morning routine; it's the best book on the subject that I know of.

Routines are about much more than mornings, of course. Take time to reflect on all the ways that good routines could help you as you navigate your typical day. Ensure your routines fit your schedule and are not overambitious. Keep them simple enough so that you can execute them consistently each and every day.

Here are a few things you can start to do now:

◎ Plan out the upcoming week over the weekend. Do this by making a list of things you want to accomplish in the upcoming week. Categorize them based on priority.

◎ Before you go to bed each night, identify and highlight three things you must do the next day to make your day productive. This will help to differentiate what is important from those things that are not as important. You will be better positioned to focus on the former first and tackle the less important later, or even delegate or outsource them if feasible.

◎ Plan out your meals for the week ahead over the weekend. Whether you cook your meals daily or buy them, planning meals ahead will save you time and money. It eliminates impulse buying because you know exactly what to buy when you go grocery shopping.

◎ Pick out your work clothes for the next day at nighttime. If you are able to, plan out what you'll wear for the entire week ahead of time.

CHAPTER 3

EXCELLENCE PRINCIPLE 2:
Commit to Growth and Improvement

COMMITMENT INVOLVES A FIRM decision or promise to do an activity, job, or project or something that you believe in. Whatever this is will require you to give of your time and energy.

Your work is a direct representation of who you are, a person of quality and integrity. So it is important that when you commit to completing a task or project, it is done well. As a matter of fact, we all should strive to give our best to whatever it is that we commit to do, even when we do things for ourselves. Be willing to go the extra mile because your work says a lot about you.

Let me share an inspiring example of commitment I encountered in my own life. Whistle Stop Desserts is a family owned bakery located in Oceanside, New York, that has been in business since 1977. This bakery is known for making a wide variety of delicious, quality desserts that include cheesecake, velvet cake, and carrot cake. These are just a few of my favorite desserts made by the bakery that I have ordered from them over the years. Some of the best, most delicious desserts that I have ever tasted have come from Whistle Stop. I have ordered custom birthday cakes for my children from them every year for over twelve years.

Do you know why I keep returning to Whistle Stop? It's their commitment to making high quality desserts. As you are already aware, I can tell quality baked goods from inferior baked goods. My years of baking have also helped me to know that you cannot make quality desserts by using inferior ingredients. Since the very first day I ordered from them, Whistle Stop has maintained their commitment to making high quality desserts, hence why I keep returning year after year.

Their commitment to consistently making high quality desserts is also what has kept them in business all of these years. They do not do any major advertisements. They do not even have an active social media presence. They simply have committed to and focused on making consistently delicious, excellent-tasting desserts that have drawn in an ever-growing and very loyal customer base. During holiday seasons, there is always a long line—sometimes over a block long!—of customers who are willing to wait to order their desserts. I once waited in line in the rain for over thirty-five minutes to order desserts for Christmas one year. As you can tell, Whistle Stop's commitment to excellence has certainly made its mark on me.

Commit to Excellence

We cannot do everything. That will stretch us thin. This is why we have to carefully consider projects and activities that we commit to. However, once we make a commitment, it is our responsibility to do that which we have committed to do to the very best of our ability.

Adopting this mindset will help you to give 100 percent on your job or project. Knowing that your work is an extension of you and a representation of you, you want to ensure that you give it your best.

As a matter of fact, the underlying premise should be, "I will leave it better than when it was committed to me." This is how you prove that you are efficient and can be trusted, and that you have the capacity for more and bigger responsibilities.

Most people would simply "manage" the project-assigned responsibilities given to them, but not you. You are a person of excellence. As a result, you are going to go the extra mile.

When Bob Iger became CEO of The Walt Disney Company in 2005, it was a challenging time for the company. In his book, *The Journey of a Lifetime*, Iger stated that his vision came down to three clear ideas: recommit to the concept that quality matters, embrace technology instead of fighting it, and think bigger—globally—and turn Disney into a stronger brand in international markets.

His commitment to the vision paid off massively. Under Iger's leadership, Disney's value grew to nearly five times what it was. Today, Disney is not just an amusement park where dreams come to life. Iger transformed it into one of the largest, most admired media companies in the world, counting Pixar, Marvel, Lucasfilm, and 21st Century Fox among its properties.

When Bob Iger handed the reins over to Bob Chapek, he left the company in a much better position than it was when he started. What a remarkable example of commitment!

As it turned out, Chapek was removed after two years and Bob Iger was called upon to lead Disney once again. As Iger's story demonstrates, do all you can to become the best at what you do and good things will result.

Invest in Yourself

You have to consistently invest in yourself, be it via enrolling in courses, training, listening to educational podcasts, reading books, or by whatever means suit you. This is part of your lifelong commitment to grow as a person. You can also learn a great deal from others, especially those who have mastered the art of their craft.

These are just a few of the ways that you can make whatever is committed into your hands grow and thrive. It is not enough to just manage the responsibility. What separates you from the rest of the pack and what makes you a person of excellence is that you look for ways to make what you are responsible for thrive.

When I worked with students and adult learners as a certified writing specialist (yes, I have worn many hats in my short lifetime), I went in with the mindset of transforming my students into excellent writers. Many times, I went beyond the call of duty.

In addition to learning to improve their writing skills, my students also learned organization and study skills. Our writing sessions often turned into Excellence Coaching sessions afterwards. I am proud to report that all my students improved their writing skills greatly under my tutelage. Most also learned a thing or two about the importance of the pursuit of excellence.

The most unusual pattern developed when I worked with my writing clients. I would usually start off working with one child and then, after a few weeks, the parents would ask if I could work with the child's sibling. This happened with four different families. In one case, I started off working with one student and by the end of the year I was working with the student, his sibling, and their mother.

I found out later on, unknown to me then, that the parents of my students took notice as I worked with their children. I was simply doing my job, going the extra mile and putting 100 percent into working with these young learners. I was also fully committed and intentional about seeing them improve greatly. For me it was a no-brainer. My responsibility was to help my students become better writers and improve their critical thinking skills. The parents took notice that I went above and beyond in helping my students improve their writing skills, and this led to me exponentially—and effortlessly!—growing my customer base and business.

Excellence pays great dividends!

I am also reminded of the story of Daniel from Biblical times. He exemplifies this principle very well. Though an exile in Babylon, he also happened to be one of the senior officials in the king's palace. He carried out his work duties with such a commitment to excellence that the king, his boss, planned to promote him as leader over the entire kingdom. (See Daniel 6: 1-3.)

Excellence has not always been my modus operandi. As a matter of fact, far from it. At one time, I also belonged to the group that did the barest minimum at work and had no desire for self-improvement or personal development. Investing in myself was furthest from my mind. If I had not lost my job during the Great Recession of 2009, I probably would have continued down that path. Even though losing my job and everything else that came with the loss was very painful, in retrospect, I am glad that it happened. It was the wake-up call that I needed to jumpstart my journey toward excellence.

It took almost eleven years for me to come to the realization that if I had not lost my job at the height of the Great Recession of 2009, I would not have been motivated to grow in excellence. While sharing the story about my excellence journey on a podcast a few years ago, I was asked if I was grateful I went through what I went through to get to where I am today. Honestly, I had not really given much thought to it before then. That was such a trying and traumatic season for me and my family that I was glad we made it through and that it was well behind us.

That unexpected question led to me not only revisiting that period of my life, but to also pull the lessons gained from that season. Now I can confidently say that I am glad I went through all that I went through back then, because it led to me discovering and growing in excellence.

Circumstances of life will not always line up in our favor. However, that should not prevent us from doing our best and doing our work with excellence. Remember the underlying premise of excellence? If you are faithful with little, more will be given to you.

Irrespective of where you are now, prove that you are dependable, that you can be relied upon and trusted, by committing to give your best to the task at hand. Commit yourself to ongoing growth and improvement. This in essence will help you expand your capacity for greater assignments, build your character, and sharpen your efficiency. Your circumstances will not always be fair or clear, but do not give too much thought to that. Focus instead on giving your best and doing your best. In no time you will reap the rewards of your dedication and commitment to excellence in the work that you are doing. Trust the process.

KEY POINTS

◎ Your work is a direct representation of who you are. So it is important that when you commit to completing a task or project, it is done well.

◎ You cannot do everything, so carefully consider each project or opportunity that comes your way before committing to it.

◎ Do all you can to become the best at what you do.

- ◎ We have a responsibility to do our very best for that which we have committed to do.

- ◎ Excellence pays great dividends!

- ◎ Circumstances of life will not always line up in our favor. However, that should not prevent us from doing our work with excellence.

- ◎ Irrespective of where you are now, prove that you can be relied upon and trusted by committing to give your best to the task at hand.

- ◎ Your underlying premise should always be, "I will leave it better than when it was committed to me."

TAKE ACTION

If you are of the mindset of "Oh, it's just a job" or "Well, they are not paying me enough," and that is why you are doing the barest minimum at work, I implore you to change that mindset.

You never know who is watching you. It could be someone who has the power to help you move to that next level. What do they see when watching you do your job, handle that project, or attend to those responsibilities committed into your care?

Do they see a hard worker doing their work with passion? Or do they see someone doing their job begrudgingly or even lazily? If the latter, please keep this in mind: even if the person watching you has the power to recommend you for a promotion, they would not because of your poor work ethic and wrong attitude toward work.

Have a renewed mindset toward whatever has been committed into your care, even if it is "only" volunteer work or "just" part-time work. Decide today to do it with excellence. In due time, your diligence and commitment to excellence will pay off and reward you with big dividends.

CHAPTER 4

EXCELLENCE PRINCIPLE 3:
Practice Gratitude

CHARLES DICKENS SENDS US all a much needed reminder in his famous quote on gratitude: "Reflect upon your present blessings—of which every man has many—not on your past misfortunes, of which all men have some."

Gratitude is a thankful appreciation for what one receives, whether tangible or intangible. When we practice gratitude, we are more likely to focus on the good things in our lives, an attitude which can foster the achievement of excellence in many ways.

Gratitude can help you develop a positive mindset, which can help you overcome obstacles and achieve your goals. When you focus on the good in your life, you are less likely to be held back by negative thoughts or emotions. Gratitude can also help motivate you to achieve your goals. When you are grateful for what you have, you are more likely to work hard to maintain it or improve upon it.

Gratitude can help you develop resilience, which is the ability to bounce back from setbacks. When you embrace and practice gratitude, you are better equipped to deal with life's challenges. Finally, embracing and practicing gratitude can help improve your relationships with others. When you are grateful for the people in your life, you are more likely to treat them with kindness and respect, which can help strengthen your relationships.

Research studies have shown how gratitude is essential to our well-being.

Two psychologists, Dr. Robert A. Emmons of the University of California, Davis, and Dr. Michael E. McCullough of the University of Miami, have conducted a great deal of research on gratitude. In one study, they asked all participants to write a few sentences each week, focusing on particular topics.[2]

One group wrote about things they were grateful for that had occurred during the week. A second group wrote about daily irritations or things that had displeased them. And the third group wrote about events that had affected them (with no emphasis on them being positive or negative).

After ten weeks, those who wrote about gratitude were more optimistic and felt better about their lives. Surprisingly, they also exercised more and had fewer visits to physicians than those who focused on sources of aggravation.

The study also noted that the improvement in physical activities also helped improve the participants' outlook on life as a whole.

In another study, Joel Wong and Joshua Brown, professors of psychology at Indiana University, carried out research on the benefits of gratitude for people who struggle with mental health concerns.[3] The study consisted of 300 university students seeking mental health counseling for depression or anxiety.

Findings from the study suggest that practicing gratitude is beneficial not just for healthy, well-adjusted individuals, but also for those who struggle with mental health concerns. They found that practicing gratitude coupled with receiving psychological counseling carry greater benefits than counseling alone, even when that gratitude practice is brief.

The results from the aforementioned studies show that gratitude should definitely be a part of everyone's daily routine (see chapter 2 for the importance of routines).

Develop a Gratitude Routine

My client Sandy reached out to me because she wanted to make a career switch. She hated her current job, which she was over-qualified for. She felt it was sucking the life out of her. After my initial consultation with Sandy, it was clear that a switch in careers was long overdue. However, she still needed to hold on to her current job because it was her only source of income. Her bosses were not the nicest, which made matters worse.

As I helped Sandy develop a plan to facilitate her career switch, it became clear to me that developing some sort of gratitude routine would be very helpful for her. So I asked her to write down ten things about her current job that she was grateful for. It took her a few days to come up with the list, but she was even able to come up with twelve things, much to her own surprise.

Sandy meditated on the list during her quiet time daily. Doing so helped to change her mindset toward her job. Over time, she found that her current job was not as bad as she initially thought. Her focus had shifted from all of the things she hated about her job to what she actually liked about her current role. This shift in focus made going into work daily so much easier. She kept the list handy and whenever she was having a difficult day at work she pulled it out and reviewed it. It prevented her from making a drastic decision that she would later regret. Focusing on this gratitude list helped Sandy to not only hold onto her job, but perform it with a great attitude and excellence as she pursued her career change.

When Sandy finally made her career switch, she admitted that creating the gratitude list helped her tremendously. She immediately started to create a new gratitude list within a week of starting her new role.

Bob Proctor, positive mindset expert coach and author, stated in one of his interviews that every day he writes down ten things that he is thankful for. He starts off every gratitude item with: "I am so happy and grateful that . . ." Doing this daily, it's no wonder he lived a full, long, and impactful life. He passed away in 2022 at the age of 87. However, his work and legacy still live on.

Speaking from personal experience, engaging in a daily gratitude routine—be it via journaling or reflecting on what I am grateful for—helps to set the tone for the day. This habit of practicing gratitude also helps to get my mind going in the right direction as I start my day.

Gratitude has been a part of my daily routine for many years now. It is also a core part of my coaching program, as gratitude is a major contributor to sustaining habits of excellence. I strongly encourage all of my coaching clients to keep a daily gratitude journal so they have a way of recording their many blessings and can reflect on those blessings later on as well.

Life is indeed complex and at times filled with seasons of difficulties. However complexities and difficult seasons of life can coexist when we embrace and practice gratitude.

May we never get to the point where we see only the things that are wrong and not working in our lives. That is a terrible and sad place to be. Irrespective of how bad the situation or circumstances are, if you look deep enough, you will find at least one thing to be thankful for.

Practicing daily gratitude has helped me to now consistently notice and appreciate the beauty and magnificence in nature. I now relish things I never used to pay the slightest attention to: sounds of rustling leaves on the trees in the late spring and summer months; the smell of a warm summer morning; the chirping of different birds; sometimes the rhythm formed by the nonstop pecking sounds of the woodpecker. I never noticed or even paid attention to any of these wonderful aspects of nature before. Practicing gratitude allows one to be still long enough to notice and hear the beautiful sounds all around.

A Simple Gratitude Practice

Here is a simple way to practice gratitude: In the morning, set aside five to ten minutes of quiet time. Close your eyes and intentionally start to reflect on different areas of life. Write down what you are thankful for as it comes to you.

I do this almost every day and it is a game changer! I suggest you do this in the morning, as this helps to set the tone for the day. But if time permits, do this also in the evening right before you go to sleep. You cannot put a price on falling asleep with a smile of contentment on your face as you reflect on all that you are thankful for.

This practice also helps to cultivate mindfulness. We live in a fast-paced world. If you live in New York, where I have lived for the past twenty-one years, everyone is always hurrying somewhere. I got this same feeling as a young university student interning at Marsh and McLennan, a global financial services corporation in London. I remember walking to work from the train station at Aldgate and always having to walk faster so as to keep up with the fast-moving Central London crowd.

The truth is, living life at this pace gets exhausting after a while, and being in perpetual fast mode can easily lead to burn out.

Practicing being still, even if it is for five minutes every morning, and recalling the things you are grateful for and then writing them down is a very therapeutic antidote.

Try it for yourself and see.

I now realize that each day is a gift that must never be wasted. I no longer take time for granted. I strive to use my time effectively daily. Why? I realize how truly privileged and blessed I am to be alive in this day and age.

In a world filled with a lot of negativity, gratitude can help us become more attuned to positivity.

The Many Benefits of Gratitude

The intentional practice of gratitude produces many positive results in life, results which contribute to one's pursuit of excellence.

For example, gratitude helps improve sleep. Cultivating gratitude throughout the day nurtures more positive thoughts that can help you drift into a more peaceful sleep.

Researchers from the University of Manchester in England examined the correlation between gratitude and sleep quality. Included in the study were 401 adults between 18 to 68 years old. Among the participants, 40 percent were recorded to have clinically impaired sleep or sleeping disorders, based on their **Pittsburgh Sleep Quality Index (PSQI)** score. By using a cross-sectional questionnaire, the researchers discovered that practicing gratitude drives negative thoughts away, especially if done soon before bedtime, thus making more room for positive thoughts and reflections that contribute to a more peaceful and longer uninterrupted slumber.[4]

Another benefit of gratitude is that it makes us less materialistic. The relentless pursuit of material things offers nothing more than instant and short-term gratification, which leads to the craving for still more. Practicing gratitude brings the focus toward intangible but more valuable things in life that contribute to overall well-being, such as accomplishing goals, fostering healthy relationships, nurturing career growth, maintaining a positive outlook in life, and more.[5]

Everything may not be perfect in your life, but instead of zeroing in on all of the things that are not working, why not instead choose to practice gratitude? By doing so you are not ignoring or undermining what you are going through or dealing with, you are just intentionally choosing to focus on the things that are working, the good things in your life.

In gratitude, you'll find little blessings even in the midst of chaos and adversity.

Why is this key? Because what we focus on magnifies over time. When we focus solely on everything wrong and not working in our lives, it leads us down a spiraling path of negativity. We then do nothing but complain, and we fail to see or even notice things that are working. Sadly, we fail to recognize the beauty all around us.

An attitude of gratitude will elevate your perspective. You'll start to see things from a higher plane. You will have an eagle's view over your life's issues. That puts you in a better position to come up with solutions. By flying at a high altitude, you allow your mind to see beyond your problems and discover previously unseen solutions.

How do you adopt a lifestyle of gratitude?

One way which I briefly touched on is by keeping a gratitude journal. Do so even on "off" days, on days when gratitude is the last thing on your mind and you feel as though you have absolutely nothing to be grateful for, and all that could possibly go wrong has gone wrong.

On such days, write something in your gratitude journal. Or perhaps review past entries. You then get a chance to see all of the great things that have happened over time and what you have overcome. After flipping through several pages of your gratitude journal, it will take you no time at all to realize that you do indeed have a lot to be grateful for, which will help to boost your mood.

KEY POINTS

◎ Gratitude is essential to our well being. It is a thankful appreciation for what an individual receives, whether tangible or intangible.

◎ The complexities and difficult seasons of life can most certainly coexist with gratitude.

◎ Irrespective of how bad the situation or circumstances are, if you look deep enough, you will find at least one thing to be thankful for.

◎ There are so many ways of practicing gratitude. Choose the method that works best for you and incorporate it into your daily routine. Be consistent.

◎ Journaling is a favorite and common method of practicing gratitude. Write down at least three things you are grateful for daily.

◎ Start and end each day with gratitude.

◎ You cannot put a price on falling asleep with a smile of contentment on your face as you reflect on all that you are thankful for.

◎ Practicing gratitude brings the focus toward intangible but more valuable things in life that contribute to your overall well-being.

◎ On days when it is so hard to even find one thing to be grateful for, reviewing your gratitude journal is greatly suggested.

◎ An attitude of gratitude will elevate your perspective on life's problems, and its opportunities.

TAKE ACTION

Practice gratitude by adding it to your daily routine. During your quiet time in the morning, write down what you are grateful for. Close out each day by writing down things that happened during the day that you are grateful for. It is especially important to do this on those difficult days when it feels like you have nothing to give thanks for. Try your hardest to write down something you are grateful for, irrespective of how unimportant or minuscule it seems.

This process will be easier and more meaningful if you have a dedicated daily gratitude journal or notebook that you will enjoy opening up and referring to when the mood strikes.

Whether you do it weekly or monthly, it is important to review your gratitude journal regularly, because it serves as a great reminder that we all have so much to be grateful for.

CHAPTER 5

EXCELLENCE PRINCIPLE 4:
Practice Appreciation

APPRECIATION IS THE ACT of showing that you are grateful to someone. It is a vital attribute to develop and a key excellence principle; it's also a wonderful way to support others in their pursuit of excellence. When we show appreciation to others, it can be a powerful tool for motivating others to strive for excellence. By showing appreciation, we are in essence saying "You are doing a great job. I see it. You are making a difference, and I am avowing it by this act of appreciation."

Appreciation and gratitude are often used interchangeably. However, there is a difference between the two words. You can easily show gratitude for a kind deed done to you or for you by simply saying thank you. For example, someone holds the door open for you at the gym. You then show your gratitude by thanking them right there and then.

Appreciation, on the other hand, moves beyond gratitude. When you show appreciation for a kind deed done, you take a specific action beyond saying thank you. There is an act involved. Gift giving is usually the act involved when we show our appreciation for a kind deed done.

I can show appreciation to a diligent coworker who goes the extra mile time and time again by sending her a thank you card and presenting her with a gift basket. Keep in mind that this is in addition to my having extended my gratitude for her diligent hard work by simply thanking her on numerous occasions in the past.

We are grateful first, then we show appreciation. In essence you can say appreciation is taking gratitude to the next level. So master gratitude, make it a part of your daily routine, and then add appreciation to the mix. You can cultivate the habit of showing appreciation by backing your gratitude with specific action and doing this often.

Remember the Whistle Stop Desserts highlighted in chapter 3? Lisa is the lead cake designer there, and she has been for as long as we have ordered birthday cakes from Whistle Stop (over twelve years now). Whenever I go in to order a custom birthday cake, Lisa always asks about my children and she somehow remembers the different cakes she has made for them over the years. As I mentioned in chapter 3, the bakery is always busy. So it never ceases to amaze me that Lisa remembers such details whenever I go there to order a birthday cake, which is usually but once or twice a year. Every single cake she has designed for us has been a hit!

In September of last year, I went to Whistle Stop to order a custom birthday cake for my youngest son. I decided to show my appreciation to Lisa for making such delicious and beautiful custom cakes for my family over the years. I did this by giving her a purse made by a luxurious, renowned brand. I sent the gift with my husband on the day of the birthday party when he went to pick up the cake. Well, the following year when I went in to place my order for another birthday cake, Lisa remembered the gift and thanked me profusely. She even ran into the back to bring the bag out to show me that she has been using it since she received it. My intention was to show my appreciation to Lisa for her commitment to excellence and for making such delicious cakes over the years. For Lisa, my token of appreciation meant the world to her and affirmed that people see and appreciate her hard work and effort.

In this digital age, you can show your appreciation by high-lighting an establishment and a worker there on your social media pages. It goes a long way.

Let's look at some other examples of expressing appreciation:

The next time you are in a restaurant and you receive out-standing service, leave a generous tip and let the manager know that the waitress did a magnificent job. This is what showing appreciation looks like.

I make it a point to give a thank you card that I address personally, along with a gift, to every guest that I interview on my "Ways of Excellence" podcast on YouTube.

When you give an end-of-year gift to your child's teacher, you are not just expressing your gratitude to the teacher, you are showing your appreciation to him for being a great teacher.

When you are moved and touched by a kind deed and then you take action to show how much the kind or good deed meant to you, you are showing appreciation.

Let's further explore the differences between gratitude and appreciation. The table below depicts a few of the major differences.

Differences between Gratitude and Appreciation

Gratitude	Appreciation
You are the main benefactor	Other people are the benefactors
You use your speech to show gratitude by immediately acknowledging that you are grateful for something done to you. Usually done by saying "thanks" or "thank you."	You show appreciation by taking action. For example, you write an email or even send a thank you card. You can even give a gift to show your appreciation.
You can be grateful for inanimate things. You can very easily give thanks for good weather, finding the perfect parking spot at the busy theme park, great health, a good night's sleep, and more.	Appreciation is an act usually done unto other humans.
Usually done on the go. Saying a quick thank you to the person who held the door for you on the way out of the gym.	Most times require careful planning and thought. For instance, buying a card or deciding on the type of gift to give.

You have probably heard the expression, "Give people their flowers while they are still alive." It means to show love and appreciation to the people in our lives while they are still living. Let them know you care and that they matter greatly to you by taking action now.

When we show appreciation, we increase the value and self-worth of the person we are appreciating. We do this by letting them know that their good work has not gone unnoticed. You also in turn encourage and give them hope.

The truth is everyone is fighting unseen battles. Even the most confident of individuals often question if they are making a difference or if their hard work matters at all. We all sometimes question if it's all worth it.

Your show of appreciation could just be the nod of affirmation a person needs to let them know that the work they are doing is making a big difference. Your act of appreciation has the power to give the person on the receiving end the confirmation they need to keep doing what they are doing, and to let them know that you see them, you care deeply, they matter, and are making a positive difference in a big way. Do not hold back on showing your appreciation to those who deserve and have earned it.

When you are on the receiving end of an act of appreciation, be sure to thank the giver and reciprocate by cultivating the habit of showing appreciation to others. Showing appreciation to others can be contagious and can lead to a positive cycle of appreciation. It can also improve our relationships with others and our own self-value.

KEY POINTS

◎ Appreciation is the act of showing that you are grateful to someone.

◎ When you show appreciation for a kind deed done, you take a specific action beyond saying thank you.

◎ There is a difference between gratitude and appreciation. *We* benefit from gratitude. *Others* benefit from our act of appreciation.

◎ We are grateful first; then we show appreciation.

◎ Appreciation is taking gratitude to the next level.

◎ When we show appreciation, we increase the value and self-worth of the person we are appreciating.

◎ Your show of appreciation could just be the nod of affirmation a person needs.

◎ Master gratitude, make it a part of your daily routine, and then add appreciation to the mix.

◎ Appreciation is usually backed by action, often in the form of gift giving.

◎ Appreciate the people in your life now. Do not wait until they are dead to appreciate them in the form of an eulogy at their funeral.

TAKE ACTION

Are there people in your life who you need to appreciate? Make a list of those people and take the time to think of how you will show your deep appreciation for all they have done. Do not rush this process, as you want to appreciate each individual properly with intention. Perhaps plan to show appreciation to one such person each week, until you have completed your list.

The next time you receive outstanding service worthy of appreciation, if say from a restaurant for example, take the extra five minutes from your schedule to let the manager know how great the waiting staff was. Take the extra time to let the chef know that the meal you just ate was very appetizing.

Let the dentist or owner of your dental practice know that the hygienist did a marvelous job.

Get into the habit of leaving reviews. Most people only leave reviews when things do not go their way or they had a bad experience. Be the exception. Show your appreciation by leaving a positive review for that business.

It's been said that charity starts at home. Show your thoughtful appreciation to your immediate and extended family members. Think of small gifts you can give or acts of kindness you can show them.

Practice showing appreciation regularly. Everyone extends gratitude for a good deed. But you are not everyone. You are a person of excellence. Differentiate yourself from the masses by showing appreciation regularly.

CHAPTER 6

EXCELLENCE PRINCIPLE 5:
Practice Tact

THE MERRIAM-WEBSTER DICTIONARY DEFINES tact as having a keen sense of knowing what to do or say in order to maintain good relations with others or avoid offense. You cannot describe yourself as a person of excellence and not know what it means to operate in tact. Excellence and tact go hand in hand.

Tact is centered around maintaining an observant understanding of other people, and being sensitive to their opinions, beliefs, ideas, and feelings.

Tact is also doing as the occasion demands: exhibiting appropriate behavior, being sensitive to cultural differences, and acknowledging and respecting the differences.

Let me relate a personal experience about cultural tactfulness. In the summer of 2022 I traveled to Cairo, Egypt, for the first time. Cairo is a beautiful city, rich in culture and history. It is a city endowed with buildings with the most spectacular architectural designs I have ever laid eyes upon. Egypt is also a major tourist attraction. The pyramids of Giza are one of the seven wonders of the world, and rightly so. Seeing the pyramids in real life left me awestruck with amazement and wonder, pun intended.

I did my due diligence before traveling to Egypt. My research results revealed that it is a predominantly Islamic nation, with over 90 percent of its citizens identifying as Muslim.

My research also revealed that in many Arab nations, women are expected to dress conservatively. Women are expected to wear loose clothes that cover the shoulders and knees. That is the culture.

As a woman visiting an Arab country, I made it a point to abide by, honor, and respect the culture. While in Egypt, I wore conservative, loose-fitting clothes. I knew it was going to be scorching hot in Cairo in July. However, with a little bit of planning and preparation, I was able to pull together outfits for the trip that covered me up nicely and still kept me very cool and comfortable. Not only did I honor and respect the culture in Egypt, I had an amazing time. It was truly an experience of a lifetime.

When we fail to do our due diligence or outrightly ignore societal norms and rules, we cause offense to others. The freedom to express oneself, be it in fashion or in speech, should not be taken as a license to cause offense.

Tact demands that we show consideration and that we are respectful of societal norms. The all-too-common attitudes of "This is who I am," "Take me as I am," and "I will do as I please, irrespective of who gets offended" are not only tactless, but show a lack of consideration. These attitudes are also very selfish.

When we act tactlessly, we alienate others, and we push them away. That attitude will not benefit us or serve us well in any way. We will only end up making more enemies than allies in the long run.

Accommodating and respecting differences in the world we live in today is not just about operating in tact, it is a demonstration of one's personal excellence.

Tact in the Workplace

It's very simple: Treat everyone with respect.

As humans, we all desire to be valued and respected. As a result, value should be accorded to everyone. Be considerate of coworkers and be willing to make reasonable accommodations.

You may have experienced having a superior in the workplace who was insensitive to your needs and cared more about the bottom line than anything else. Think back to how that made you feel. Do not end up being that type of boss.

Listen more. I like that common expression "We have two ears and one mouth to show that we need to listen more and talk less." Interrupting every conversation or talking over everyone else because you want to get your point across is tactless.

Conversely, acknowledging others *is* a sign of tact. Taking the extra second or two to acknowledge the recipient or recipients of the text or email you are sending, show that you value them as human beings first over the task or assignment that you want them to do. This can be accomplished by simply inserting a greeting before their name: "Hello, Jane," "Good morning, Ada," "Hi, Dan, trust all is well."

In today's fast-paced world, it is as though we have somehow all forgotten how to greet. Everyone just jumps right into the message. I find that highly irritating. It is also concerning because our kids copy all that we do. They are watching. If we as adults are not displaying proper behavior, the next generation will equally follow suit.

Even saying thank you for a good deed or gift is fast becoming a lost art. That is a real shame. And it is especially important in the workplace, where one frequently needs to build up the goodwill of colleagues in order to effectively do one's job.

Acknowledging the receipt of the gift at the moment is saying thank you. Sending a thank you card, an email, or a text message afterward leaves a lasting memorable impression and is an act of appreciation.

I was a guest on a podcast a few years ago. This was around the time of the release of my first book, *Joab, King David's Top General: Essential Lessons on Character.* Gary, the host of the podcast, was gracious during the interview. To my utmost surprise, he sent a box of cookies and brownies along with a handwritten thank you note about a week after he interviewed me.

Out of the several podcasts I was on during that season, his kind gesture is what I remember most vividly. For you it might not be cookies, but think of the one unique way you could thank others for their kindness.

In today's fast-paced world, tact is embodied in intentionally slowing down and being present. Where are we all rushing too anyway? Proper planning and time management will eliminate the need to always be in a rush, as though we are all vying for some first place prize for the fastest rusher.

Tact encompasses many things, including emotional intelligence, respect, discretion, self-awareness , thoughtfulness, compassion, subtlety, honesty, diplomacy, courtesy, and patience.

When we act in tact we command respect; we show that we care for and value others. In the workplace, the person who operates with tactfulness is often viewed as a team player, and is correspondingly rewarded.

Communicating with Tact

Communicating with tact is showing respect and consideration for the other person's feelings as we convey our message. It involves paying close attention to *what* (words) we say and *how* (body language and tone) we say it so as not to offend.

Communicating with tact is a skill that is mastered over time with much practice and intentionality. It is an essential skill because it fosters effective communication. When we communicate with tact, we are able to preserve relationships, build credibility, and demonstrate thoughtfulness.

Here is a wonderful principle of tact that we all should strive to abide by: I may not agree with your views or perspective on a lot of things, but it is still my intention to accord you respect and honor as a fellow human.

As a nation, we need a return to this principle. Our differences in political views and affiliations do not justify acting tactlessly toward one another. We should still be able to respect and honor one another irrespective of our differences.

Other Examples of Tact

Say Thank You

Your lack of tact could be costing you more than you realize. For example, are you sure to always send a thank you email after interviews?

A friend shared with me recently that she narrowed down candidates for a director position at her company to two equally strong candidates that she interviewed. She was having a hard time deciding between the two. Do you know what the deciding factor was for her? You guessed it: the thank you email. The candidate that did not bother to send a thank you email after the interview just missed out on a great opportunity.

Thank you emails should not just be limited to job interviews. Let's normalize sending thank you notes, cards, and messages, and making thank you phone calls, to show the depth of our appreciation.

Always thank guests for gifts and for attending your event. Let's get back to the days of sending thank you notes, or even making a phone call to thank guests for coming out to celebrate a birthday, graduation, or any event. At the very least, send a text message to thank them for coming and for the gifts. This gesture should not be limited to weddings only. It should be a must-do on every post-event agenda.

Gifts Count

While on that topic, please be tactful. Do not show up to some-one's birthday party without a gift, especially a child's event. For young children, the gifts matter more than anything else. For kids, birthday parties are synonymous to Santa showing up on Christmas day with a bunch of presents. At the very least, bring a gift card.

A friend organized a small birthday party for her child one summer. She invited about seven kids altogether. She told me that out of the seven kids invited, only three or four brought gifts. Needless to say, her child was distraught at not getting gifts from all of her friends on her birthday. Her parents felt awful!

Children are wired differently. Yes, they want their friends to come celebrate with them on their special day. But the real icing on top of the cake is the opening of the presents after the big event. Can you just imagine how disappointing it must have been for that young child to realize that over half of those invited to her party did not even bother to bring a gift. If you are a parent, you would hate to see that look of disappointment and hurt on your child's face. Please do not do that to someone else's child.

Your tactfulness should extend to adults, too. If you can plan ahead of time to be at someone's party, you can most certainly plan ahead to get the hostess or celebrant a gift.

It shows a lack of decorum and tact when we are invited to an event and show up without a gift. So yes, let us normalize getting a gift for the host/hostess, celebrants, and, especially, young kids.

The Yoruba tribe of Nigeria believe that you show the depth of your appreciation by thanking a person up until the third day for their act of kindness or largesse. I believe that's an attitude we all should consider adopting.

RSVP for Events Promptly

RSVP to let the host know whether or not you will be able to attend their event. The event organizer needs to receive that information in a timely manner to plan accordingly. RSVPs do not apply only to when you can make an event. If you are unable to attend, let them know as well. It is the courteous thing to do.

After you RSVP to let them know that you are coming, do show up. I recently read a story about a couple that invited eighty-eight people to their wedding and not even forty of those who said they were going to be there showed up. This tactless act ended up costing the couple thousands of dollars. So much food went to waste. There were several empty tables, festooned with beautiful handmade favors the bride had spent so much time putting together for her wedding guests. She was saddled with close to fifty pieces of favors meant for guests who had RSVPed earlier to say they would attend the wedding but then did not show up on the day of the event.

You can just imagine how this couple must have felt on their wedding day. Sadly, this is not an isolated experience. The comments section of the article revealed that others have experienced similar fates.

Return the Shopping Cart

Please put the shopping cart back where it belongs. To all you people who leave carts in the middle of a parking spot or in the middle of the road in a shopping center, I have been wanting to ask this question for a long time: What planet are you from? You were able to go get the cart, but then putting it back after using it is now a problem? Put yourself in the shoes of the person who has to go around the shopping center picking up after you? What if that was your child or even grandchild? Or elderly grandparent? Yes, I have seen a few elderly individuals collecting shopping carts in shopping centers, sometimes under inclement weather conditions. Would you still abandon your empty cart in the middle of the shopping center if they were relatives of yours?

As you can see, so much of tactfulness dovetails with common courtesy. Do unto others as you would want them to do unto you.

Also keep in mind that how we do a thing is how we do *every*thing. If you belong to the club of those that abandon carts in parking spots and in the middle of the shopping center, that speaks volumes about you! What else do you do?

That mindset and behavior will permeate other areas of life without you even realizing it. We do better when we know better. Kindly put your shopping cart back in the right place when you are done shopping and unloading the cart. It is the right, proper, and tactful thing to do.

And people of excellence are always tactful.

Be Respectful of the Cultures and Beliefs of Other Countries

Show tact and respect if you are a visitor or tourist in a foreign country. If their age-long beliefs and culture are fully acceptable to the natives and do not hurt or harm anyone, it is not your place to go there and try to change or disparage those beliefs.

A few examples: If you plan on visiting a country like Egypt, where women cover their heads in public, but you do not do so in your own country, the tactful thing to do is to abide by the hosting country's societal rules while you are there.

In Japan, for example, shoes are not worn inside the house. Well, if you happen to visit a Japanese family or go to Japan, out of respect for those you are visiting (even if your own custom varies), do not wear shoes inside their house.

The proper, courteous, and respectful thing to do is to respect the culture of the country you are visiting. This of course means that you would have done your due diligence to learn as much as you can about the culture and societal rules (written and unwritten) of where you are going.

Extend this respect to your own community. In the checkout line at the grocery store, be kind enough to put the divider on the checkout counter belt for the person behind you, once you are done loading your items onto the belt. It is the tactful thing to do.

Similarly, at the gym, wipe down the equipment after you use it, and return your weights back to where they belong. Put the dumbbells back so others can use them.

As you can see, tact requires mindfulness and awareness. These various qualities work together to help you grow in excellence.

KEY POINTS

◎ Tact is having a keen sense of what to do or say in order to maintain good relations with others or avoid offense.

◎ Tact is doing as the occasion demands. Being sensitive to cultural differences, acknowledging and respecting those differences.

◎ Communicating with tact is showing respect and consideration for the other person's feelings as we convey our message.

◎ Tact demands that we show consideration and that we are respectful of societal norms.

◎ Accommodating and respecting differences in the world we live in today is not just about operating in tact, it is an example of personal excellence.

◎ When we practice tact, we command respect, and we show that we care for and value others.

◎ How we communicate is far more important than what we communicate.

◎ Communicating with tact is a skill that is mastered over time with much practice and intentionality.

○ Our differences in political affiliations or beliefs do not justify acting tactlessly toward one another. We should still be able to respect one another.

○ People of excellence operate in tact.

TAKE ACTION

Start every correspondence, be it a text or email, with a greeting or an acknowledgment of the recipient. This small detail shows that you value the person on the receiving end much more than the message or request you are trying to convey.

As you go about your day, carry out simple acts of tact such as:

○ Returning the shopping cart back to its rightful place after you unload it.

○ When you go grocery shopping, get into the habit of putting items you do not want back where they belong. Or give the items to the cashier when checking out so they can ensure they are returned to the proper location.

○ Honor policies such as not wearing shoes inside the house when visiting others. Do not give your hosts a difficult time about it. It's their house, which means you must abide by their rules and policies.

○ Show respect and honor for other cultures when visiting foreign countries. Take the time to learn about what the acceptable behavior is in that land so as to be able to fully respect and honor the culture.

◎ Take care of your yard and the immediate surroundings of your place of residence.

◎ Communicate with work colleagues respectfully and with kindness.

Embracing and practicing tact at its very core is simply treating others with respect and kindness. This is a fundamental human need.

CHAPTER 7

EXCELLENCE PRINCIPLE 6:
Your Relationships Matter Greatly

RELATIONSHIPS ARE GREAT, AND they make our lives fuller. In fact, it's hard to imagine life without relationships. However, at times they can be complex and sometimes trying. Yet in all that complexity lies beauty and so much more.

No one was created to live as an island, irrespective of how introverted the person is or how independent they are. We all need people. This is why it is important to learn and master people skills, so as to get along with those we are in community with, be it at work, home, neighborhood, and more.

The people we spend the most time with shape who we become. When we spend enough time with anyone, soon enough we start to talk like them, think like them, copy their mannerisms, behave like they behave, and so on. If relationships have that much influence on us, then it isn't it wise for us to be selective about who we spend most of our time with?

Here's how relationships tie into excellence: It's been said that we adopt the perception, life views, attitude, and lifestyle of the five people we spend the most time with. The late Jim Rohn, renowned motivational speaker and author, famously said, "You are the average of the five people you spend the most time with." If that's the case, should you prioritize people who bring out the best in you? Who motivates you to be the most excellent version of yourself?

The truth is, it is hard to resist influence, hence why we have to be so very selective about who we allow into our sphere of influence. The optimal goal is to be surrounded by people who will help us move forward in life and not hold us back. We should strive to be surrounded by people who challenge us.

I am going to assume you have a great dream for your future. If so, and you look around you and realize that the people in your life are small-minded in their thinking—or even worse, they have no future goals or ambitions—how will that affect you? In order for you to realize your audacious goals and dreams, you will need to change friends. You will need to surround yourself with like-minded new friends who will challenge you to actualize your goals and dreams.

We become like the people we choose to expose ourselves to. You can accelerate your personal growth by spending time around people who you want to become, by either spending time with them physically, if the opportunity presents itself, or even virtually.

In the virtual sense, you can surround yourself with those you want to emulate by reading their books, following them on social media, and listening to their podcasts. When they organize public events, make it a point to attend the event.

Another great way to mesh such individuals into your life is to support their work. You do this by supporting their charity, their business, or even sowing into their lives directly. Sowing does not always have to be monetary. If the opportunity presents itself, pay for their dinner. You can also sow your time and support their work.

According to research carried out by human motivation expert and Harvard psychologist Dr. David McClelland, people who we spend the most time with determine as much as 95 percent of our success or failure in life.[6]

Here are a few strategies to help you to achieve excellence in your relationships:

Beware of Pessimists and Doomsayers

The same goes for individuals who have nothing but complaints to offer when they talk, or those who always see the glass half empty. Avoid them! As a matter of fact, I consider such people toxic! Spend as little time with them as possible. They have conditioned their minds to see the bad and never the good in anything. They always worsen any problem by finding fault with everyone and everything. They are quick to criticize but never seem to have solutions for anything. The problem is always everyone else's but theirs. Not only are such individuals toxic, they have a way of draining you of your emotional energy. Spending time around them is exhausting and demotivating. Get away!

Hurt Will Happen

As long as you are on this planet, people will step on your toes. And you will do the same, even if unknowingly. In order words, hurt will happen! There is no escaping or avoiding that. To walk in relationship excellence, you must learn to quickly forgive and let offenses go. Let them roll off you like water off a duck's back. This is not to say issues are not to be addressed. But learn to choose your battles wisely. Let go of the small issues. It is just not worth wasting your limited emotional energy over them. Save your emotional energy for the things that truly count!

Another way of not letting everything get to you is to be mentally prepared to overlook little offenses such as being cut off in traffic. Or being triggered by the tactless coworker or the cantankerous neighbor. You have control over yourself, but you cannot control others. You cannot control what they say and their actions. The best we can do is be good examples, but we cannot change others. So there's no point stressing unnecessarily over it.

When you are insulted, be quick to forgive and forget it, for you are virtuous when you overlook an offense. In other words, you show you are a person of high moral standards and character when you choose to overlook a minor aggression or rudeness.

I once had a client who lacked tact and writing etiquette. I would get text messages at all hours in the morning and there was never any form of greeting or acknowledgment in them, which I find very irritating. I always replied to the client's messages with a greeting and "Hope all is well" or "How are you?", hoping that the client would realize that it is courteous and shows decorum on their part to greet or at the very least include a simple hello at the beginning of texts and email.

The client chose not to reciprocate and continued to send correspondence via text and email without the greetings. I really could not change that and so I learned to just ignore their lack of decorum. I did have to set firm boundaries with the timing of the text messages though. I did not appreciate receiving text messages at ungodly hours of the morning. I share more on the importance of boundaries in relationships below.

Boundaries

Boundaries are limits or guidelines that you put in place to protect your mental health, values, identity, and responsibilities from being compromised or violated by others. They apply to how we live out our lives daily, and how we teach others how to treat us.

Boundaries are necessary in relationships, and it is important to set and announce what those boundaries are to others very early on, and then to abide by those boundaries.

It is no good announcing to coworkers that they should refrain from using curse words in your presence, but then whenever you are on the phone you curse like a sailor. That is being hypocritical!

You cannot tell your board members not to gossip when you do exactly the same thing. Just the same way that you cannot announce to others that you do not engage in gossip, but then every time you turn around you are always speaking ill of others (which, by the way, is gossip).

Boundaries in relationships are necessary to protect our overall well-being. In your different relationships, establish boundaries, announce them, and keep them.

For example, Sundays are a no-working day for me. All of my clients know this, so they know not to ask to schedule one-on-one coaching sessions on Sundays. It is just not going to happen. Sunday is my Sabbath, my day of rest and worship.

When you do not define boundaries in your various relationships and clearly communicate them, it leads to confusion and offense. A person may unknowingly cross your boundary line, causing you to be angry and upset. However, it will be no fault of theirs because they had no prior knowledge of the boundary. This is why it is key to announce boundaries. If you do not want your boundaries violated, be sure to clearly communicate them to others and live them out.

Cultivate Relationships

It has been said that your net worth is your network. I recently watched a documentary by Tayo Aina Films. It gave a peek into what it looks like to spend twenty-four hours with African musical megastar Davido. My biggest takeaway from the documentary was that Davido's inner circle consisted of people who ensured the megastar's music business runs like a well-oiled machine. Most of the members of his inner circle have been with him for over ten years, even before he became the world-renowned superstar that he is today.

This buttresses my point about the importance of cultivating relationships that matter to you. You do so by intentionally carving out time in your schedule for those who truly matter, irrespective of how busy you are. If they are truly important to you, you will make the time for them. Just like you need to take proper care of a houseplant in order for it to flourish, you need to take care of your relationships in order for them to flourish.

I decided a while back to rearrange my schedule on Fridays so I have some free time to get together for lunch or brunch with my friends. My friends and I are all very busy moms. It is usually challenging to connect outside of midweek phone calls because most of them work full-time jobs in addition to taking care of their families. The majority, though, have schedules that let up a bit on Fridays, so leveraging Fridays has allowed me to spend more time with them. Our lunches usually last for about two hours, and during that time we really get to connect and bond. I put the time and energy into cultivating these relationships because, like a houseplant, they bring joy and color to my life.

If you are married, this is even more of an imperative. It is so very easy to get used to seeing each other all the time that the

82

marriage is set permanently on cruise control without either of you realizing it. It is impossible for any marriage to thrive that way.

Intentionality is required. Go out on dates like you used to before you got married. They do not have to be expensive dates either. I personally do not like eating out all the time. I like to know what goes into my food. Plus, I have had enough food poisoning episodes to last me a lifetime. My husband knows this. We both love the outdoors, so sometimes our dates involve hiking, walking through an arboretum, or visiting a preserve. And sometimes we do eat out too. He loves to eat out and is very adventurous when it comes to food. So compromise is required. We have found a nice area of compromise that works for us, and we run with that.

Do not wait until a major occurrence to realize you should have been more intentional with your marriage. Do so now!

Communication

Communication is key in any relationship. Some people like to talk more than others. You have to find a way to tactfully communicate your feelings to others. I have found that nine out of ten times, when issues are discussed, they are resolved. Airing out the issue helps to illuminate and resolve the miscommunication or misunderstanding. Most people do not like confrontations. Truth be told, talking about issues can be awkward and difficult, but at times it is necessary and can save a relationship from an unnecessary demise. Discussing a problem with the goal of resolution is a far better option than sweeping it under the rug and letting resentment build and fester.

Strive to discuss issues irrespective of how difficult the conversation may be. If after you have spoken to the individual and they are still proving difficult, at least you know you tried. You have satisfied your conscience, and at that point you let them be. We cannot control everything and we should not even try.

Some friendships last a lifetime. Some for a season, some for several seasons. I have had all of the aforementioned types of relationships. Be discerning enough to know when a relationship is ordained for just a season. Do not try to turn such a relationship into a lifetime. It takes two to be in a relationship. If the season of a particular relationship is over, then let it be. No hard feelings, be thankful for the times and beautiful memories. Sometimes as we grow and mature, our values with those we called friends no longer align and we find ourselves not having much in common with them any longer. That too is okay, and is part of life. We all evolve and change over time, especially when we become intentional with our pursuit of excellence and growth in all areas of our lives. Not all friends will wish to follow us in this pursuit.

This next point discussed below will save you from a whole lot of heartache and confusion.

Bestow the Title of Friend with Intention

It is important to understand the different categories of relationships. For example, many of us use the label and title of friend too loosely. There is a major difference between an acquaintance and a friend. There is no point according the title and privileges of a best friend upon someone who you had a great lunch with once. Just because you hit it off right there and then does not automatically make this person your best friend, or even a friend at all. They may just see you as an acquaintance and treat you as such the next time your paths cross.

Do not be so quick to bestow titles on people, especially titles they have not earned. It will save you a lot of heartache and keep you from getting disappointed.

Let a person prove that they are worthy of the title of friend through their actions before you call them one. Proving takes time. It takes time to learn about who a person truly is. Take the necessary time to study them and learn more about their character before calling them friend. Ensure the feelings are mutual. After all, it takes two to be in a relationship. You cannot determine this over coffee or a lunch date.

I have had to learn this lesson the hard way. I once worked with someone who I hit it off with immediately. I made the mistake of bestowing the title of friend on them too soon. I expected this person to act as a friend would, and was hurt and disappointed when they did not. Well, in retrospect, and now that I know better, I realized that this person considered me as a close work colleague and nothing more.

Your next-door cordial neighbor is just that until they prove otherwise. A school mom who you talk to regularly at drop-off or pickup is just that until they prove otherwise. A coworker is just that irrespective of how friendly he/she appears to be until they prove otherwise.

Putting all of the aforementioned into practice will save you a lot of heartache when it comes to knowing who your friends truly are.

Be intentional about who you keep company with. This is worth repeating. The premise behind keeping great company can be summed up in this: "He who walks with the wise will become wise, but the companion of fools will be destroyed."—Proverbs 13:20 BSB

When you choose to keep company with those who make wrong choices, even if you have no intention of becoming like them, over time you will indeed, slowly but surely, eventually become like them. This is how powerful relationships are. The erosion of good morals or character does not happen overnight, it happens gradually. Even worse, it happens subconsciously.

Those we spend the most time with shape us in many more ways than we realize. They influence our core values, the belief system from which we make decisions. We all operate from our core values, whether we realize it or not. If the core values of those you align yourself with are rooted in wisdom, integrity, and responsibility, your core values will inevitably be rooted in the same. If their core values are rooted in foolishness, laziness, irresponsibility, and other negative principles and philosophies, do not be surprised if you start to make decisions based on their negative principles and philosophies. This will inevitably lead to trouble and ultimately destruction down the road.

When it comes to who you spend your most time with, you really have to put sentiments aside. If their values do not align with yours, even if they are family, the best thing to do is to distance yourself from them and spend as little time with them as possible. Again, this is because you do not want their character, or lack thereof, corroding yours.

Do not be deceived: associating with the wrong people *will* corrupt your moral habits and ethics. Sometimes we make the excuse that we have known such individuals for as long as we have been alive, and as a result we have no choice but to spend as much time with them as possible—even when their values do not align with ours.

My question to you is this: "Will you sacrifice your life's purpose to please family and friends?"

You owe it to yourself, your purpose, and your future to wisely and diligently choose those you spend time around. When it comes to bad influences, the only choice is to spend as little time with them as possible. Be loving and cordial, but never forget that these are not people who you spend hours on end around.

How to Find Like-minded People with Goals Similar to Yours

Whenever I facilitate leadership training workshops on excellence or host seminars on the topic, I talk about the importance of choosing the right circle of influence. And I always get asked this question without fail from at least one person : "So, where does one find like-minded individuals who share similar goals to yours?"

I hope the non-exhaustive list below helps to jump-start the process of finding the right social support circle that will help you to reach your highest potential.

- ◎ Toastmasters International is a nonprofit educational organization that teaches public speaking and leadership skills through a worldwide network of clubs. Find your local chapter and you are bound to find other like-minded people at the monthly meetings.
- ◎ Meetup is a social networking platform that allows people to organize and attend events based on common interests. You can use Meetup to meet friends who share similar interests. You can even find local groups, events, and activities near you by searching for them on the Meetup platform.
- ◎ Eventbrite is a global platform for live experiences that allows anyone to create, share, find, and attend events that fuel their passions and enrich their lives.

I have used all of the aforementioned platforms and I can attest that if you find a group or event that fuels your passions on any of them and attend consistently for a period of time, you are bound to meet several driven individuals with goals similar to yours.

However, you have to be proactive at these events. Keep your intention at the forefront when you attend; you may need to go out of your comfort zone to meet people. Be sure to volunteer or assist at these events whenever possible. That is one sure way of standing out from the crowd.

Another option for meeting people is to join a mastermind group. A mastermind group is a group of people who share a common goal and who support each other to achieve it. A mastermind group offers brainstorming, education, peer accountability, and feedback to its members. The group creates a powerful force of collective knowledge and effort that can help each member overcome challenges and grow.

I joined my first mastermind group a few years ago and it was indeed a transformational experience. Business partners, multi-million dollar business ideas, and more have been born from mastermind groups. The best thing about a mastermind is that every member wants to see other members succeed, and the collective knowledge and resources from the group is unmatched.

I usually find out about masterminds via my virtual mentors, the people who I admire and follow on their different platforms for the positive impact they have made and continue to make in the world. Sometimes they even host or facilitate masterminds themselves. Other times they share information about masterminds that they recommend.

Go to where people who like to do things you like to do go. If it is reading, show up at library events. You have to be strategic and intentional and most times, you actually have to physically show up at these events to meet new people.

These are just a few of the many ways that you can meet new like-minded people. I am sure you can think of many more.

KEY POINTS

◎ The people we spend the most time with shape who we become.

◎ We adopt the perceptions, life views, attitudes, and lifestyles of the top five people we spend the most time with.

◎ The optimal goal is to surround yourself with people who will help you move forward in life, not hold you back.

◎ Do not be deceived. Having the wrong associations sooner than later will corrupt and defile your good manners, morals, and character.

◎ Boundaries in relationships are necessary to protect our overall well-being.

◎ When you do not clearly define and communicate boundaries in your various relationships, it leads to confusion and offense.

◎ In how we live out our lives daily, we teach others how to treat us.

◎ Let others prove through their actions over time that they are worthy of the title of friend before you bestow such a title on them.

◎ Some friendships last a lifetime, some for a season, some for several seasons.

◎ You owe it to yourself, your purpose, and your future to wisely and diligently choose those you spend time around.

TAKE ACTION

Answer the following questions to help you evaluate the quality of your circle of influence:

- ◎ Who are the people in your life?
- ◎ Do your goals and values align with theirs?
- ◎ Do they have goals or values worthy of emulation?
- ◎ Where do they see themselves in five years? This is where you will end up in five years as well.
- ◎ Why do you spend time with them?
- ◎ What type of person are you becoming as a result of your closest relationships?
- ◎ Do they inspire you?
- ◎ Do they motivate you? And do they encourage you to develop your greatness?
- ◎ Do they stretch you?

If your answers lean more toward the negative than the affirmative, then it is time to find a new circle of friends.

Irrespective of how long you have known them for, if your friends' goals for growth do not align with yours, then you definitely want to spend as little time with them as possible for your own good.

This is not always easy, especially if they are close family members or if you have known them all your life or for a very long time. In instances like those, strong boundaries are required.

Put sentiments aside and do what you need to do.

CHAPTER 8

EXCELLENCE PRINCIPLE 7:
Cultivating Good Character Is Vital to Excellence

AUTHOR AND PASTOR A. W. Tozer defined character as the "excellence of moral beings."

Just as the excellence of a diamond is in its purity and the excellence of a baby is in its innocence, the excellence of a person is in their character, the moral qualities distinctive to that individual.

Sadly, like tact, having good character is fast becoming a thing of the past in today's society. Not that it no longer exists at all, but it is becoming harder to come across people with great character.

Scientists agree that positive character can be learned, practiced, and cultivated. In the short but impactful eight-minute movie entitled *The Science of Character*, directed by award-winning filmmaker Tiffany Shlain, the neuroscience behind a strong character is explored. The findings show that the human character is not fixed, but rather positive character traits can be developed over time. The results from this research also revealed that when we focus on building upon the strengths that we already have, it has a lasting effect on our happiness and well-being.

Relatedly, science has shown that certain key character traits seem to enjoy universal appreciation. In their book *Character Strengths and Virtues: A Handbook and Classification*, authors Christopher Peterson and Martin Seligman detail how researchers, through their empirical studies, uncovered six broad-ranging virtues that almost every culture across the world supports: wisdom, courage, humanity, justice, temperance, and transcendence. In your own life, do you not find that you also value these qualities, both in yourself and in others?

I have included mention of these findings here because they serve as a great starting point on discovering one's character strengths and virtues, and they are a great framework for identifying other positive character traits that a person may want to adopt and cultivate over time. I encourage you to read more about this in *Character Strengths and Virtues*. And if you're interested in reading the research that underlies these findings, you find that in the paper "Positive Psychology Progress: Empirical Validation of Interventions."[7]

Other studies on character show that there are seven character strengths that facilitate academic achievement, success, and happiness, irrespective of your circumstances or geographical location. Those seven are optimism, gratitude, enthusiasm, curiosity, self-control, social intelligence, and perseverance (grit).

I have included the above research findings to help you identify character traits that you may want to develop and cultivate. If the subject of character interests you as much as it does me, you'll find a host of quality books on the topic, in addition to the books mentioned above.

Treating Others Well Is the Root of Good Character

According to Fred Kiel, author of the book *Return on Character: The Real Reason Leaders and Their Companies Win*, the way we treat other people is our character in action. I couldn't agree more.

Whenever I ask my coaching clients to name a few of their character traits during my one-on-one sessions with them, most talk about traits they desire or want. There is absolutely nothing wrong with that. However, the litmus test for who you are character-wise is best seen in how you treat other people. That is the gold standard.

You cannot say kindness is a character trait of yours but then be mean-spirited in your dealings with others. Or conduct yourself so that everyone else has to walk on eggshells when they are around you. That is definitely a major dichotomy between who you say you are and what your real character reveals. It is now up to you to do the necessary work to close the gap.

The saying "You will know a tree by its fruit" could not be more accurate. It is a metaphorical phrase that means you can judge a person by their actions or behavior. In other words, their inner character will not somehow mysteriously differ from their observable character.

Just the same way a bad tree cannot produce good fruit, a person with poor character will display actions and behavior consistent with who they are. However, if the tree is good, the fruit will also be good. A person who has done the required work of developing and adopting good character traits will effortlessly live out good character every day.

So if you want to produce good fruit, you must first work on the tree that bears it. Take good care of the tree and in no time it will start to produce an abundance of good fruit.

93

Building Character Takes Time

As simple as this sounds, becoming a person of character requires intentionality and consistency. It does not just happen automatically because we think it, wish it, or see ourselves as so. We have to work hard at becoming a person of character. The work required is to be done daily and on a consistent basis.

Several years back, I decided I wanted to be known as a person whose word is their bond. Someone who does not make excuses but lives her life in a way where people truly know that when I say I will do something or commit to a project, they can consider it as good as done. Well, unbeknown to me, when one decides to master a new positive character trait, the universe will test them time and time again! The more you fail the test, the many more times you will retake the test. It is a phenomenon that I have observed over the years, especially as I continue to study and pursue excellence in my own life and as I work with others to grow in excellence.

I cannot even tell you the number of times I was tested. Somehow, circumstances lined up where I was forced to either build and master this character trait or abandon it altogether. It was not easy but I was determined. Today, I am very selective about what I commit to. I cannot do or commit to everything. That will lead to burnout. But you can rest assured that when I say I will do a thing, I will get it done very well.

It is not always easy and sometimes it comes at a cost. However, in a world where many say yes or commit and then change their minds on a whim—often with no explanation or forewarning—I want to be the exception. In other words, you can count on me as being the reliable and dependable one.

One of the major reasons that I decided to write a biography about Joab, Israel's great army commander under the rule of King David, was because when I studied this leader and his many accomplishments, I was surprised to realize that a person or even leader can be exceptionally good at their craft or work like Joab was, yet still lack character.

Joab was an exceptionally talented army commander who played a significant role in helping the Israeli army remain undefeated during the forty-year tenure of his master, King David. Sadly, he never took the time to develop his character or even address his many personality deficiencies. As a result, there was an enormous dichotomy between who Joab was as an army commander on the battlefield and who he was when he was not doing what he did best, leading the army of Israel into battle. Outside of work, he was a vicious, wicked, downright evil individual. Tragically, he did not come to realize this until it was too late. You can read and learn about Joab and the many great lessons from his life in my book *Joab, King David's Top General: Essential Lessons on Character.*

As we develop and hone our skills, be it at work or in other areas of life, it is imperative that we take the time to develop good character traits and live them out daily. After it is all said and done, we will not be remembered for what we did but for how we treated others, which is the greatest reflection of our character.

Anything you learn can be unlearned. You can unlearn bad behavior and replace it with good behavior. In the same way you can unlearn bad character traits and master new character traits. But you want to be sure that you are clear on what exactly it is you need to learn and need to unlearn.

For example, if you want to be a person of integrity, you keep working at it. To develop it, you keep doing the right thing, even in little matters. Especially when no one is looking. This is how you develop integrity. If you do this consistently and long enough, it will become interwoven into the fiber of your being such that when you are tested on larger matters of integrity you will pass with flying colors.

We all want to be led by leaders with strong character and who are responsible for their actions. We want our children to be ethical and have strong moral values. Let's not forget that the development of character starts with you and me. Decide today to be the change that you want to see in others. Be a great example of what a person of great character looks like.

I once had a client, Paula, who reached out to me because she wanted to learn and develop habits and systems of excellence. This included learning character traits that would help her to excel in her career and relationships. From the get-go, I saw that Paula was lacking in the areas of truthfulness and integrity. We discussed these character deficits in our sessions and came up with a plan to help her unlearn these inhibiting traits and replace them with positive character traits.

Paula, however, was inconsistent in following the laid out plans. As with habits, how we do one thing is generally how we do most things. Soon enough, Paula's character deficits spilled into our working relationship. She started to delay on invoice payments with no explanations. She would ignore reminders for days on end or come up with excuses. She always had a story about why something was not done.

After several missed payments and excuses from Paula, I had no other choice but to terminate my working relationship with her. That experience taught me a major lesson. We can say we want to change as loudly as we want to and for as long as we want to; however, real change will only happen when we decide to *do* the work required for us to see the positive change that we want in our lives. But if we offer a never-ending list of excuses and reasons as to why we keep perpetuating bad behavior and bad character traits, it simply means that we are not ready for real change. Such change is just a desire or even wishful thinking at best.

A person has to get to the point where they see how inhibitive and debilitating their bad character traits are and become willing to do whatever it takes to unlearn those character traits and replace them with new and better traits. Only then can they begin the process of becoming a better version of themselves, a much-improved version of themselves that they are proud of.

Even though Paula came to me expressing that she wanted to change, sadly, it was just wishful thinking at that point. She was not ready for real change and was still very comfortable living with her limiting negative character traits.

Building character takes both willingness and time. Paula was not ready, but many of us are. Can you imagine the cascading effect of deciding to be a person of character? Imagine an entire community filled with people of character, a whole nation, a world where most of its citizens are people of character. It is not impossible. Let the change start with you. You will be surprised at the number of people you will impact with that one life-changing decision.

Character Is not Reputation

Whereas a person's character are the evident positive qualities, sound morals, and ethical principles that individual embodies, reputation on the other hand is the set of general beliefs held by others of that person.

Your reputation is how society sees you. It is external. Character is more internal. Who you are character-wise stems from your core. You can control and even change your character, but you have little to no control over your reputation, how others on the outside perceive you.

It takes a long time to cultivate and master character traits. Reputation on the other hand can be instantaneous and even fleeting. A person can gain the reputation of being a social media influencer overnight after a video goes viral, whereas developing solid, good character traits requires intentional work done over a period of time. It is reflective of the long-term pursuit of excellence, and it does not happen overnight.

There is nothing wrong with wanting others to think highly of us, but who you truly are—your character—is vastly more important. Focus on cultivating the latter.

If you are in a leadership position, it is your responsibility to ensure your team demonstrates good character. You can model that by leading by example.

Good character indeed has many great benefits, even for organizations. In *Return on Character*, Fred Kiel successfully showed through a thirty-year in-depth study that companies with leaders with good character and an executive board with the same are profitable. Such companies see a higher return on income. In other words, good character impacts the bottom line of organizations in a positive way.

You can reshape your character for the better. There is no such thing as "This is who I am and how I will always be." If you have character traits limiting your growth and success, acknowledge them, identify what exactly you need to change, and then make those changes with the help of a coach or consultant. You can do it! And the rewards for developing a character of excellence make the hard effort worth it.

KEY POINTS

◎ The excellence of a person can be found in their character.

◎ The way we treat other people is our character in action.

◎ Scientists agree that positive character traits can be learned, practiced, and cultivated.

◎ To develop character, it is necessary to take the time to identify the core values or virtues you want to have or want to be known for. Then cultivate these values so they become a part of your character.

◎ Anything you learn can be unlearned. You can unlearn bad behavior and replace it with good behavior.

◎ Just as a bad tree cannot produce good fruit, a person with poor character will display actions and behavior consistent with who they are internally.

◎ Human character is not fixed. Positive character traits can be learned, practiced, and cultivated.

◎ A person's reputation is the set of general beliefs held by others of that person. Your reputation is not your character.

◎ Your reputation is how society sees you.

◎ Good character indeed has many great benefits, even for organizations.

TAKE ACTION

How to develop great character

To develop character, it is necessary to take the time to identify the core values or virtues you want to have or want to be known for, and then cultivate these values so they become a part of your character. This is a rewarding journey, but it will take time. You will find the steps below useful in helping you to develop character traits that you desire.

◎ Take the time to write down the top five character traits that are most important to you.
   - Do an honest evaluation. Does your character as it is now reflect any of these five traits, partially or completely or even at all? You want to be as honest as possible with yourself. No sugarcoating of any kind. Be true and honest.
   - Consider asking a loved one/loved ones to contribute to this effort by honestly describing the character qualities that you live out daily.
◎ Begin the necessary work on cultivating the traits you have identified.
◎ Working with a coach is highly suggested. A good coach will not only help you see your strong areas, but will also help you work on character deficits. Their work will most certainly include helping you to cultivate the character traits you seek to develop.

This is a big part of what I do when I work with clients on a one-on-one basis.

When you regress, your coach will not only hold you accountable for your actions, but will help you to identify negative triggers and do the work required to minimize future relapses as you master new character traits.

◎   Practice makes perfect. Or in this case, it leads to making great improvements.

CHAPTER 9

EXCELLENCE PRINCIPLE 8:
Protect the Integrity of Your Heart

THE HEART IS THE epicenter of the myriad of emotions we experience daily as humans. These emotions include sadness, shock, disappointment, joy, and heartbreak, to name a few.

The heart is also the epicenter of the human character. You may have heard it said that "As your heart is, so are you." Just as a bad tree cannot yield good fruit, a heart that has been compromised by unhealed trauma and wounds will be revealed by its actions and words. It's impossible to live a life of excellence with that type of heart.

When we fail to deal with and heal from past hurt, trauma, and other emotional wounds, our words and actions usually produce unforgiveness, resentment, and bitterness among others.

It is going to be hard for a person with unhealed trauma or resentment to walk in excellence. Why? Sadly, that person's pursuit of excellence will be shrouded in the aforementioned resentment, unforgiveness, and bitterness that slowly eat away at the core of who the person truly is on the inside. These traits are like cancer. Often, their negative effects remain hidden until much later, when it may be too late to heal them.

You may think you are fine, but deep down you know you are not. You still feel slighted from what happened thirty-five years ago. Your words and actions are usually a dead giveaway!

My advice to you: get professional help. Therapy, to be exact, to help you get to the root of the issue and to deal with it. Then supplement that with life coaching with a focus on excellence development so that you are fully equipped with the support systems and processes you need to thrive and win at life. Heal your heart so you may start walking the true path you are meant to take.

I am sure you have been around people who do not see the good in anything. They see the worst in everything. When they speak, they speak with spite. You can almost feel the negative energy seeping out of every pore of their body. Sadly, they do not even realize how negative they are in their dealings with others. This is an example of how undealt-with-trauma manifests.

I was part of a group of volunteers working toward a just cause. We all got along pretty well except for one of the volunteers. She was feisty and her attitude was as though she was ever ready to attack anyone she deemed as an opponent. If you did not agree with her point of view, she made it clear through her words and actions that she viewed you as an enemy. I was left with no other choice but to confront this group member about her behavior and way of communicating, as it was starting to negatively affect the other members of the group and impact the work we were all doing. When I confronted her, she expressed surprise. She did not know that she was rubbing the other volunteers in the group the wrong way. I applied the strategies on tact found in chapter 6 during the confrontation. This approach took her off her "war footing" during our conversation. In fact, she apologized and vowed to change. Since then, it has been a night-and-day difference. She is now a totally different person, so much easier to deal with and work with.

We all have blindspots that we are unaware of. A person with a growth mindset who is perpetually pursuing excellence will be open to constructive criticism and make the necessary changes. For others, undealt with trauma and emotional wounds are like a weight, a very heavy weight to be precise. A weight so heavy that it prevents a person from living a life of excellence. Bitterness and resentment taint all that they do and say.

Cherish and Protect Your Heart

Just as a face is reflected in water, so your heart reflects the real you. What truly lies in a person's heart will in time be exposed, especially in unguarded moments or when under pressure. A person who is racist, xenophobic, homophobic, or prejudiced in any way can only conceal their true self for so long. Who they really are is often revealed in their actions and words and even body language.

This is why it is of utmost importance to pay attention to and frequently evaluate the state of our hearts with the greatest degree of honesty we can muster. In doing so, if we discover or come to the realization that we are still holding on to unforgiveness from twenty years ago, we can get the help and intervention we need to get on the right path.

The truth is, many of the times, the effects which are the by-product of our hurt heart are noticeable to all except us. The effect of undealt with issues spills over into our behavior and actions, limiting us in more ways than we realize.

This is why we have to daily guard our heart from offenses and anything else that can easily come in to corrupt or compromise its integrity. We are imperfect beings living in an imperfect world. Offenses and hurt will come, that is just inevitable. Hate and all of the other negative emotions stem from the heart. Guard your heart against such intense negative emotions and it will remain strong and whole.

How do you guard your heart?

First and foremost, what and who you expose yourself to matters greatly. Deep down, a person may know that there is hate, resentment, and bitterness in their heart. If that person now surrounds themself with likeminded people, then they are doing nothing but reinforcing that prejudice, hate, resentment, and bitterness. Misery loves company. Their friends may even validate the unhealthy behavior by saying, "It is OK to hold on to such negative emotions because of what the offender did. After all, they would do the same as well." If you find yourself in this situation, you must be true to yourself and ask yourself, "How is holding on to such negative emotions helping me? Am I truly at peace?" And then ask yourself again, "Do I really want to associate with such people who have so much negativity?" The answer is probably no, because they are a bad influence.

Be very selective about who and what you expose the gateways of your heart to. Your eyes, ears, and all other impressions and associations all directly affect the state of your heart.

Be slow to anger.

We cannot take everything to heart in the figurative sense. We have to know when to ignore rather than confront and address issues. Most of the smaller offenses must be ignored deliberately. We cannot control how others act, but we can certainly control our actions, reactions, and responses to them.

Learn to Forgive

When you choose to deliberately ignore offenses or even forgive, you are doing it for you. You are doing it because you know that the weight of unforgiveness, resentment, bitterness, jealousy, and the like is ridiculously heavy and will hinder your pursuit of a life of excellence.

Don't let the offender steal any more from you. It's not always easy to let go or forgive, but the cost of carrying the weight of unforgiveness and hurt or resentment is just too high.

A while back, I watched a documentary about the parents of the young children who died in the Sandy Hook Massacre. The documentary aired about five years after the event. The Sandy Hook Elementary School shooting was a mass shooting that occurred on December 14, 2012, in Newtown, Connecticut, United States, when 20-year-old Adam Lanza shot and killed twenty-six people. Twenty of the victims were children between six and seven years old. Lanza then turned the gun on himself, fatally shooting himself in the head after he had murdered the first grade students and their teachers.

I was particularly taken aback by one of the mothers of the murdered students. She made the difficult decision to forgive the mentally ill shooter for taking the life of her only son under such incomprehensibly gruesome circumstances. The bereaved mother said that she chose to forgive the shooter so that she could move on with her life. She realized that if she instead had chosen not to forgive Adam Lanza, she would have felt like she was being bound in chains to him and forced to take him with her everywhere she went, even though he was dead.

She went on to say that the pain and grief of losing her only child will remain with her forever, but she knew that if she did not make the decision to forgive the shooter, he would not only succeed in robbing her of her young beloved child, but he would succeed in robbing her of her own life as well.

Choosing not to forgive the shooter was costing her too much. She wanted to continue to live her life for the sake of her son, she said. She also wanted to do a lot of work to bring awareness to gun violence, but she realized she could not when she held onto the unforgiveness. The weight of the unforgiveness was too heavy and incapacitating. She went on to say that her son, even though he was no longer with her physically, would want her to continue to live her life, even after the devastating loss she had experienced.

This woman chose life. She chose not to let the shooter rob her of her future. This was her way of protecting what remained of her badly hurt heart.

I am not saying this is easy. I also have an eight-year-old son who brings so much joy into our lives with his bubbly personality and kind, generous heart. The thought of losing him under such horrific circumstances is truly unthinkable and makes writing this story exceptionally difficult.

Forgiveness is not an easy process. As a matter of fact, to completely forgive a person is a process that for some people has to happen over and over and over again. Not everyone is quick to forgive. Also, different studies suggest that certain personality types find it harder to forgive than others.

I learned in therapy years ago that it is okay to forgive many times over. If you have to forgive a person ten times before you can fully and truly forgive them, then do what you must. If the forgiving process is a continuous process for you, then so be it. Keep in mind that this is for you. Do all you can in your power to ensure that the poison of unforgiveness does not remain in you. Get that deadly toxin out of you and get it out as fast as you can. Otherwise, it will corrode the integrity of your heart.

From experience, I can tell you firsthand that as you practice living in a continual state of forgiveness, it becomes easier and easier to forgive and overlook offenses. You need to build and strengthen your forgiveness muscles starting today by practicing forgiveness and letting go.

You are doing it for you and not the perpetrator. It is only when we strip off the weights that slow us down and prevent us from living a life of excellence that we can soar in excellence. It is also then that we can experience true lasting peace.

Let peace be the ultimate goal always.

Be at peace with yourself and your decisions, and then do your best to live at peace with everyone else. Some people are not for peace; you cannot control that. But you probably have some degree of control over how much you interact with them, and you most certainly can control your own decisions and actions.

Peace at times comes at a high cost. The high cost can be in the form of forgiving the unforgivable. The Sandy Hook mom chose peace in her decision to forgive. She cut off the hold the perpetrator had on her.

The truth is this: a mind tormented with thoughts of revenge and what ifs is not a mind at peace. Forgiving others allows us to experience peace, true inner peace. You cannot put a price on that. Again, when you choose to forgive, you are doing it for you, for your well-being, and not for the offender.

Perhaps the offenders never apologized or are no longer even alive. But you are still here and you deserve to live your life unencumbered with the weight of unforgiveness and hurt. So forgive them.

Choosing to forgive is choosing to live and not letting the act and the perpetrator rob you of your future. In the Take Action section at the end of this chapter is a forgiveness exercise that will help you to get the junk of unforgiveness out of your heart and mind. This exercise is a process and system of continual release through forgiveness of the offender. It is a simple but powerful exercise that gets the job done.

Do it as many times as necessary. Be very honest and be as vulnerable as you need to when carrying out this exercise. You are doing it for you, for your own freedom, and not for anyone else. You owe yourself that much.

All of my coaching clients carry out this forgiveness exercise. Why? Because it will be next to impossible to arrive at a place of authentic healing while holding on and carrying the heavy weight of unforgiveness. I implore you to carry out this exercise. It is truly liberating. Do it as many times as you need to for as many people as you need to. If it takes you days or even weeks, that is fine.

KEY POINTS

◎ The heart is the epicenter of the myriad of emotions we experience daily as humans.

◎ When we fail to deal with and heal from past hurt, trauma, and other emotional wounds, the effect will be unforgiveness, resentment, and bitterness, to name a few.

◎ Undealt with trauma and emotional wounds are like a heavy weight that prevent a person from living a life of excellence.

◎ We are imperfect beings living in an imperfect world. Offenses and hurt will come; that is just inevitable.

◎ We cannot control how others act, but we can certainly control our actions, reactions, and responses to others.

◎ Forgiveness is not an easy process. As a matter of fact, to completely forgive a person is a process that for some people has to happen over and over and over again.

◎ Let peace be the ultimate goal always. Seek peace with yourself and your decisions and then do your best to live at peace with everyone else.

◎ Peace at times comes at a high cost. The high cost can be in the form of forgiving the unforgivable.

◎ Forgiving others allows us to experience peace, true inner peace.

◎ Choosing to forgive is choosing to live and not letting the act and the perpetrator rob you of your future.

TAKE ACTION

Forgiveness exercise

You will need:

◎ Several sheets of lined paper

◎ A pen

◎ A quiet private space.

The steps:

1. Each sheet is for each person that you want to forgive.
2. On each sheet, write down the name of who you want to forgive. That will be the heading.
3. Then on each line write down what they did to hurt you. Be detailed.
4. Get it all out on paper. This part can be difficult.
5. A lot of times we may have buried the offense deep into our subconscious, but it is important to get it all out on paper during this exercise in order for healing to occur.
6. Once you have filled your sheet with the offenses, you then say this out loud: "I forgive you for_____."
7. Then you read out what they did to you line by line with no omission.
8. Once that is done, and you are sure you have it all on paper, you then tear up the sheets of paper and burn them.
9. There you have it. You did it. You have forgiven the offender and you have taken physical actions to show your willingness to forgive.
10. Be sure to do this for as many people that you need to forgive.
11. Do not rush through this exercise. Be true and thorough as you carry it out.

Trust me, it works. My clients have all found this forgiveness exercise very useful and helpful. And I have had to carry out this exercise a few times myself. We are all human and hurt is inevitable; forgiveness allows us to heal and move forward in life.

The only requirements: be truthful, be detailed, and be vulnerable as you work through this forgiveness exercise. You are not sharing it with anyone. And always go back to the purpose for why you are doing this when you find it hard to continue with the exercise: to break free from the stronghold of unforgiveness. You owe it to yourself to live a free, purposeful life of excellence.

When the memories of the offense come up—and sometimes they will—always go back to this exercise. Remind yourself that you have done what you needed to to forgive the offender.

If you need to enlist the help of a coach to help you with this forgiveness exercise, then do so. The ultimate goal here is to get the poisonous toxins of unforgiveness out of your system. Treat it like cancer. Remove it.

CHAPTER 10

EXCELLENCE PRINCIPLE 9: PRACTICE GENEROSITY

WHEN WE GIVE OF our resources, we create the capacity for more to flow into our lives. This is a principle that many of the biggest philanthropists on the planet know very well. Their giving to others expands the fullness of their own lives.

Some of the wealthiest in the world are also some of the biggest givers. Billionaire Sidney E. Frank was the founder of Grey Goose Vodka. This vodka has been credited as the best-tasting vodka in the world. He was seventy-five years old when he came up with the idea for Grey Goose. In a mere seven years he was able to sell Grey Goose to Bacardi for $2 billion. Former United States president Donald Trump described Sidney Frank as the most generous man he has ever met.

Sidney Frank was not born into great wealth. In fact, he was so poor that he had to drop out of Brown University after his first year of college because he could not afford the tuition. Later in his life, to ensure that another Brown University student would never experience what happened to him, Sidney Frank donated $100 million in financial aid to the poorest students at Brown.

That is just one of many stories about Frank's charitable giving. He cared deeply about others and wanted to help others avoid the privation he experienced as a young college student. He gave much more to his alma mater after that initial donation. Before he died, he willed all of his money to a charity foundation run by his daughter. He died in 2006, a philanthropic role model who left a legacy of bountiful generosity.

Dr. Paul Osteen, brother to megachurch pastor and multi-time *New York Times* best-selling author Joel Osteen, spends five months out of the year in the remote areas of Zambia in Africa performing surgery on very sick poor patients for free. He gave up his very successful medical practice in Arkansas to do this mission work. His main reason for doing so? He said in an interview, "Over three billion people in the world do not have access to great medical care, and that just does not not sit well with me." So he chose to do something about it.

You do not have to reach billionaire status like Sidney Frank or be a surgeon like Dr. Paul Osteen to become a giver. Start where you are and with what you have now. It could be volunteering at your child's school Parent Teacher Association events. Sign up to become a volunteer at your local senior center or youth center. You can start off with a few hours a week and increase it from there.

Whenever we give, we create the room to receive more into our lives and are able to continually give from that place of abundance. It is a deeply nourishing feedback loop, and this scripture explains the principle well: "If you give to others, you will be given a full amount in return. It will be packed down, shaken together, and spilling over into your lap. The way you treat others is the way you will be treated."—Luke 6:38

Make giving consistently to others a part of your financial plan. We do not give when we feel like it, or when we are moved emotionally by an advertisement about starving children in a war-ravaged part of the world. We give because it is the right thing to do and it is the secret to lasting prosperity.

Excellence and generosity are not mutually exclusive. They are, in fact, profoundly supportive of each other. Generosity is among the many strands that form the tapestry of excellence.

You will be hard-pressed to find a person of excellence who does not have a generous spirit. Generosity is a fruit of excellence. It is simply giving out of the abundance of what you have been given. A lot of times it looks and feels like we do not have anything to give. The truth is we all have something to give. It doesn't always have to be monetary. We can give of our time, knowledge, and so much more.

The Relationship between Generosity and Kindness

Kindness is generally thought of as the quality of being friendly, considerate, and compassionate. It is the act of showing goodwill, even in small ways. Kindness involves paying attention to the people around us and acting with a sense of warmth and care. People who are kind act that way not for any reward or even recognition, but because it is the right way to behave and the way a person wishes others would act toward them. I am sure you have heard of the popular term "acts of kindness."

Acts of kindness simply involve doing something nice for someone else, without them asking and without you doing it for anything in return. Examples of acts of kindness include:

◎ Smiling. It costs nothing and you can brighten someone's day just by smiling warmly and genuinely at them.
◎ Giving up your seat on public transport to someone who might need it more.
◎ Holding the door for the person behind you.
◎ Helping a stranger.
◎ Being patient with others.

Acts of kindness may be small, but they make a significant impact. Generosity on the other hand goes beyond what is necessary or expected. It is the act of giving to others in a way that goes past what is usual or required. It involves helping others and providing support, often materially. It involves giving freely and abundantly without expecting anything in return. Acts of generosity are usually more visible and are sometimes publicly recognized. A generous act can also have a broader and more long-term effect that can potentially change circumstances and address larger needs, as we saw in the example of Frank Sidney with his philanthropic donations to Brown University.

Examples of acts of generosity include:

◎ Donating a cash prize to a school
◎ Helping a friend move into a new apartment
◎ Helping your elderly next-door neighbor do their grocery shopping
◎ Paying vet fees to neuter and release your neighborhood's stray cats
◎ Paying for the coffee of the person in line behind you.

Generosity has the power to transform the heart of the giver for the better. Studies have shown that carrying out acts of generosity has a calming effect on our hearts.

In one study, participants were asked to picture their mother and tell her how much they love and appreciate her. The researchers found that the heart rates of the participants decreased significantly compared to other participants in the study who did not partake in the exercise.[8] In summary, practicing kindness and generosity not only warms our hearts emotionally, it also has tangible benefits for our physical health.

Generosity is having an overall spirit of kindness. A kind word can lift spirits, while a generous act can change lives. In some religions and cultures, generosity and kindness are considered virtues. Both acts of kindness and generosity have the power to transform our world for the better in major ways.

Give with the Right Attitude

Giving is the gift that never gets old. In fact, the more we give to one another, the better we feel all around. It is one of the beautiful ways we can express our affection and appreciation to people we care about, and sometimes even to perfect strangers. A kind-hearted gesture can have an incredible impact, and it can even start an amazing chain reaction of people paying the gesture forward.

A person who gives freely, loves freely, and lives life with no hidden agenda or ulterior motives has realized over time that we give because we have been blessed with so much. In a miraculous way, being generous with our resources leads to fulfillment and having even more. I believe that generosity helps us to overcome the innate insatiable nature within us to always acquire more. We conquer that by being generous.

When we give of our resources, we are essentially sowing a seed which will come back to us multiplied in the ten, hundred, and even thousandfold. Give of your time, your skills, and your expertise. Volunteer. Do pro bono work. The truth is there is never a perfect time to give. You have to be intentional and consistent about giving. Get those seeds in the ground now; your future will thank you for it.

We recently toured the Great Smoky Mountains in Tennessee. We learned from our tour guide, Phil, that the Great Smoky Mountains National Park is one of the few remaining free national parks in the United States. The park administrators rely solely on volunteers and donations to keep the park running.

Phil is one of those volunteers. He had a garbage bag in tow during our tour. Whenever we stopped for photos or to explore a major landmark on the mountains, he always looked around to see if there was any litter. If he spotted any, he diligently picked it up. I later saw other tour guides doing the same, as well as some volunteers removing graffiti from the short walls along the park's road. None of these people were paid a salary; they derived satisfaction from ensuring the Smoky Mountains park was clean and well preserved for the hundreds of thousands of people who visit annually—not to mention the over 1500 black bears that call the Smoky Mountains home.

I thought to myself, if we all played our small part in keeping our neighborhoods clean, being our brothers' keeper, being mindful of the animals that we share this space called Earth with, what a truly wonderful world this planet would be! We would definitely not have to worry about a lot of the issues that we are facing now. Creating a world like that can start with you and me today.

Another thing that struck me about the Smoky Mountain volunteers was how happy and delightful they all were doing free work. They smiled and had a great attitude about them. Phil is one of the best tour guides we have had to date. He was friendly and went above and beyond during our four-hour tour.

The attitude with which you give matters greatly. Do not give under compulsion or begrudgingly. The best givers are cheerful givers with great attitudes. They live a lifestyle of generosity and they love it.

If you decide to make generosity a part of your routine and life, please be one of the cheerful givers. If you decide to volunteer at a museum or at a PTA event, smile often and be a part of the solution, not the problem.

Generosity in Action: Abenity

I first heard of Brian Roland, founder of Abenity, when he was a guest on one of my favorite podcasts. His company is revolutionizing how organizations approach perks by making them accessible, transparent, and impactful for everyone they serve. In the podcast, Brian shared about his company's charitable giving. I was blown away by the intentionality behind their generosity.

Here is how he describes it: "Before we made our first dollar, we committed 15 percent of net earnings toward the biggest problem we could think of, extreme poverty. We labeled our social mission 'Perks with Purpose,' and we began sponsoring children through World Vision in alignment with the United Nations' number one goal of eradicating extreme poverty for all people everywhere by the year 2030." To date, Abenity's impact fund has provided over $1 million of support toward efforts to eradicate extreme poverty by the year 2030.

I am not surprised that Abenity is a successful corporation. They are helping their customers, other companies, via the work that they do, and at the same time they are impacting and changing lives through their charitable work.

The projects they have supported provide countless children with access to clean water and education for life. They have equipped accountable entrepreneurs with micro-finance capital to acquire key resources, including goats, chickens, refrigeration, bicycles, and sewing machines. They are also sponsoring more than 245 children every month, meeting their basic needs for nutrition, healthcare, and education.

Toward the end of his interview, Brian Roland said: "Here's the bottom line. You're never going to regret choosing to become more generous."

Brian is a phenomenal example of a leader who understands and practices the principle of being generous. Generous people give out of their resources because they care deeply about their just causes. What is your just cause?

In November of 2022, I attended my first Parent Teacher Association convention in Albany, New York. Yes, I am a proud PTA mom. I was also elected co-president of my local PTA unit in 2023.

The convention was such a great event and experience! But even more so, I was amazed by all of the volunteers who gave of their time and expertise to make the convention happen. The majority of the volunteers, mostly women, hold full-time jobs. They are business owners, career women, and have families. They face life issues daily like the rest of us. But yet they still generously take time out of their busy schedules to be fully involved in the PTA. At the schools where they serve, many of the volunteers are charged with fundraising, planning fun events for the students and other members of their school community, advocating for the welfare of students, ensuring students have all of the resources and support they need to excel—and the list goes on and on.

At that event, I listened as the executive board members of New York state's PTA detailed how they travel frequently to the highest offices of the land advocating for students in New York state. They did not have to. Just like the rest of us, they are super-busy women and men who wear ten different hats, but they still choose to give of their time and other resources regularly.

To some, being generous comes naturally. It is intrinsic to them. Others have to work harder at it. It really does not make much of a difference. Knowing yourself and doing your part is what truly matters when it comes to practicing generosity.

Watch Out for Freeloaders

A word of caution: As you walk in generosity, be mindful of free-loaders. They have no limits and no boundaries. They are only interested in getting as many freebies as they can. They are usually very stingy with their time and resources, and have a mentality of just taking and taking from others. Always full of excuses, they can never make the time to give of their time or resources unless it benefits them in some way or they are going to get something back.

Mark them and be firm with them. If they need help and you are able to, help them. But do not let a freeloader mistake your kind-heartedness and generosity for weakness, or ever think it is okay to take as much as they can from you. Be sure you have clearly set boundaries when dealing with such individuals. Circle back to chapter 7, where I discuss the importance of setting the right boundaries in relationships.

Give for the right motive.

Let the motive be right. Always check your motive. Always ask yourself: "Am I doing this for the right reasons? Am I hoping to get something back?"

Ensure you are giving for the right reasons and with the right motive always.

A parent said to me recently that she joined the PTA of her daughter's school because she wanted to be a voice for her daughter, who had been bullied previously and had had a few unpleasant experiences at school. That is a great example of giving of one's time for a just cause and the right reason.

We cannot solve all of the problems in the world, and, yes, we will always have the poor with us. But can you just imagine a world where almost all of us cared an awful lot about different causes and, like Brian Roland and Sidney Frank, actually did something about it? Guess what would happen then? A whole lot of things would get better. Poverty in the world would be greatly reduced, amongst many other wonderful things.

It is truly more blessed to give than to receive. You are not just making a difference in the life of another, but you are blessing your soul in the process. There is an amazing, indescribable, wonderful feeling that bubbles up from the very depth of our souls when we give.

Make giving a lifestyle. Sow great seeds of generosity. Your future self will thank you for it.

KEY POINTS

◎ When we give of our resources, we create the capacity for more to flow into our lives.

◎ We give because it is the right thing to do and it is the secret to lasting prosperity.

◎ Generosity is a fruit of excellence. It is simply giving out of the abundance of what you have been given.

◎ A generous person gives without expecting anything in return. Giving is the gift that never gets old.

◎ When we give of our resources, we are essentially sowing a seed which will come back to us multiplied in the ten, hundred, and even thousandfold.

◎ The attitude with which you give matters greatly. Do not give under compulsion or begrudgingly. The best givers are cheerful givers with great attitudes.

◎ Generous people give out of their resources because they care deeply about their just cause. What is your just cause?

◎ As you walk in generosity, be mindful of freeloaders. They have no limits and no boundaries.

◎ Ensure you are giving for the right reasons and with the right motive always.

◎ Carrying out acts of generosity is gratifying for the soul.

TAKE ACTION

Think of how you can start walking in generosity today. Start by looking around you. Where can you give of your time and resources in your community? If you have children, a good place to start is by joining your local PTA and actively participating by volunteering at events.

Make financial giving a consistent part of your financial plan. Find a charity, foundation, or just cause that you believe in and that you can give to regularly. Give monthly or bi-weekly. Whatever works for you. Give what you can afford. The goal is to be consistent.

Get into the habit of displaying random acts of kindness. Smile more and genuinely. When you see something out of place, in say a supermarket for example, put it in the right place. Whenever I find meat or vegetables in an aisle where they don't belong, if it was just put there, I will put it back or give it to the store workers. Compliment someone you see today. Let someone skip you in the checkout line if they have just a handful of items compared to you. Give a hug to someone who needs it. Call or text someone you haven't spoken to in a while and ask how they are doing.

CHAPTER 11

EXCELLENCE PRINCIPLE 10:
Master Your Personal Finances

IF YOU WERE TO lose your job or main source of income today, do you have enough to cover your living expenses for the next couple of months until you find a new job? Even if that job search takes anywhere from three to six months?

The truth is, there is no difference between a person who earns a high six-figure salary and someone who earns $45,000 a year if both lack financial discipline, have no savings, and have no financial cushion to fall back on in hard times. Both of them will be in the same financial deep hole due to their lack of financial discipline should a sudden job loss occur.

You may have heard it said that "What good is money in the hands of a fool if he has no intention of getting wisdom?"—Proverbs 17:16

In other words, a person has no business desiring to own or handle abundant money if the desire to learn how to master financial excellence is not there.

Sadly, personal financial management skills are not taught in a lot of schools. Even with an MBA degree, it was not until I hit rock bottom financially that I was forced to learn from the experts. The personal finance management strategies that I share here have contributed greatly toward setting me on the path of financial discipline and financial excellence. And financial excellence is a powerful ally undergirding all your efforts toward personal excellence.

If you are familiar with the strategies in this chapter and have not implemented them yet, let them serve as a much-needed reminder to you to get started. And if you are already implementing several of these strategies, I am certain there will be at least one if not more that you will need to tighten or change after reading through this material. All of that is to say, do not rush through this section so as not to miss out on the wealth of information and financial wisdom it contains.

Learn the Science of Budgeting

Spend less than you earn.

As simple as this sounds, a multitude of studies and reports show that the majority spend more than they earn and rely on credit to make up the difference. Spending more than you earn is very unwise. When you spend more than you earn, you are living beyond your means.

I hear this all the time from my clients: "I have too many bills." If you say the same, here is my question to you: Who created the bills? The reason why you are struggling to pay your bills is because you simply have not mastered financial excellence in your personal finances. You are probably spending more than you earn. Evaluate your spending habits to cut out whatever is unnecessary. Look for ways to reduce your bills. You probably have monthly subscriptions that you no longer use, so cancel them.

Some people are conditioned to spending all that they earn or living paycheck to paycheck. During my personal finance illiteracy days, that is exactly what I did. I spent most of what I earned, since I would be receiving another check in two weeks. I did this for many years. I spent money on the most frivolous things. Living that way is living in the danger zone! It is also a fast path to financial insolvency.

When I did eventually lose my job, I found myself in a truly hopeless situation. If your current spending habit looks anything like mine once did, take this as a loud clarion call for you to STOP! You can do better. Continue reading to find out how.

What you really need is a budget. Yes, I know it is not everyone's favorite word. But a budget is a necessary and crucial tool to help you accurately identify your monthly expenses and to ensure that those expenses are way below your monthly income. It is really the only system that I know of that can help you get a clear visual for how much you are bringing in and spending monthly, and from there how to allocate those funds. Setting up a simple budget will help to ensure you have enough and are not spending more than you earn. Without a budget, you might run out of money before your next paycheck. You most likely will.

Budget systems have come a long way. There are so many applications that you can use. Most are free and can be found easily online. Or if you are old school like me, use good old Excel spreadsheets. Even those can be automated so that all you have to do is enter in the numbers. Then the program does all the hard work of calculating for you. With some simple research on the internet, you will find an easy-to-use budget system that works for you.

In the initial stages of using a budget, you will need to regularly evaluate your results to ensure you are on track to meet your financial goals. You can do this by comparing the actual numbers with your budgeted numbers to see if there are any differences or variances. This analysis will inform you on how to then make the necessary corrections. If, for instance, you budgeted $100 for groceries for the week but spent $150, you will be able to see this discrepancy during your budget review. You then need to decide if you need to reduce your future grocery expenses to match your budget, or instead modify your budget to match your actual expenses—or perhaps use a combination of the two approaches. This will apply to all spending categories in your budget.

To see change in your finances you have to make the necessary moves. Take the right steps toward reshaping your budget so that it fits your income and works for you. Spending all that you earn or even more than you earn is what gets many into financial trouble. And on top of that, in today's economy there is no such thing as job security. What if the checks stop coming in due to a job loss, as happened to me? Or if your income craters due to illness or injury, as we see with so many professional athletes who do not handle their finances wisely. It is not a good position to be in. Having a simple budget and applying the strategies highlighted below will help you to avoid a similar fate.

Save, Give, and Invest

Save

Whether we like it or not, emergencies are a part of life and happen to us all: the unexpectedly expensive car repair, the house boiler breaking down, an unexpected medical bill, or a pet needing emergency surgery. The list of examples goes on and on. Having an emergency fund will help to ensure you are well-prepared for life's emergencies.

You can even easily set up this fund through your bank. Or you can set it up yourself online. Configure it so that a set amount of money is deducted automatically from every paycheck that goes into the emergency fund account.

Having separate funds for vacations and holidays is also a smart move. Putting an expensive vacation on your credit card with the hopes of paying it off later is being financially reckless. Again, what if you stop working or are unable to pay off the credit card debt due to reasons beyond your control? A better way to go on vacations stress free is to gradually build up a separate fund for vacation expenses, and plan for major vacations months in advance. Save toward the vacation over time using the same method highlighted for putting money into your emergencies account.

Give

Giving should be a consistent part of your personal finance regimen. You may want to pause here to go back and reread chapter 10 on generosity. Giving comes in many forms, be it tithing 10 percent of your income to your church, or consistently giving 10 percent of your income (or any amount you feel comfortable with) to your favorite charity, or even setting aside an amount monthly that goes toward giving in general. Again, you can set this up automatically through your bank so that a set amount is taken out at every paycheck.

> "There is one who scatters, and increases yet more. There is one who withholds more than is appropriate, but gains poverty."—Proverbs 11:24

This pretty much sums up the mystery behind the principle of giving, and explains why everyone should be a giver.

Adopt a Different Perspective on Debt

I was born in Nigeria and lived there until my early teen years. Growing up, I saw my parents and their friends save up (sometimes for years) to acquire assets. Houses were built from the ground up, and that took several years. But irrespective of how long it took, once you are done building the house, it is yours and there is no mortgage to worry about. My family lived in a rented apartment until my parents were able to build their first home.

I share the story about my parents because it's important to consider developing a different mindset about debt. Yes, I understand that in the Western world, getting a mortgage or large loans is about the only way one can buy a house. But hearing stories about how it's done in other parts of the world can inspire and lead to the emergence of new ideas when it comes to using debt to finance large purchases.

It was not until I moved to England that I really had my first introduction to making huge purchases, such as financing a house on credit. Fast forward to 2001 when I relocated to the United States. I was shocked to see how easy it was to access borrowed money on credit cards. I noticed that ease of credit access was greatly amplified, but the costs attached were rarely talked about.

Call me old school, but I have always been wary of making large purchases on borrowed money. As a matter of fact, the idea of using borrowed money to buy most material goods still baffles me, most especially when it comes to fast-depreciating items like furniture, appliances, etc. Even after all these years, making purchases using a credit card is still very much a foreign concept to me. Credit cards have their place. For example, they offer some protection, especially in cases where the seller fails to deliver the product or service promised. That's why I use credit cards to buy airline tickets, book hotels, and rent vehicles. However, I always make sure that the money to pay it back is already there. I don't use borrowed money to pay for things. It is not my style. We are all very different; I am simply sharing what has worked for me and kept me and my family out of debt.

Here is the sad truth about debt: those who borrow are slaves of moneylenders. When you owe, you are bound to the lender in many more ways than you realize until you fully pay off your debt. The same applies to mortgages. Your major life decisions are impacted by the debt you owe. This is why I strongly advise to carry as little debt as possible.

But debt is generally unavoidable when it comes to purchasing a house. So be sure you are ready mentally and financially before you take on a mortgage. The ownership and upkeep of a house is very expensive. On Long Island, New York, where I live, the average cost of a moderate house is around $650,000. Most of the houses around here were built in the early 1900s. When you buy a house in my area, expect to spend a small fortune renovating it to your taste. That is not the type of debt you want to take on casually, especially if you are not ready financially. It might be wiser to rent and save up substantially to purchase a home in the future.

When you consider a mortgage, carefully do your due diligence. Weigh the pros and cons well before you make such a huge commitment. I know a lady who purchased a house with her older children. The house required a great deal of work. Unfortunately, they had poured all of their savings into the purchase of the house, so there is very little money available to make the much-needed repairs. That is what you call being house poor.

Being house broke or house poor means you're spending too much on housing expenses relative to your income. This leaves little money left for other necessities, such as savings, giving, and paying other bills. It can result in a cascading accumulation of debt, accrued simply by spending the necessary amount to cover daily living expenses. Being house poor usually means resorting to using credit cards to cover living expenses.

Avoid becoming house poor by all means. It is not worth it. That is no way to live. Your quality of life should be better than that.

I recently watched an interview where Coco Gauff, the 2023 US Open Women's Tennis Champion, was asked if she was going to use her $3 million winning check to pay off her debts. She laughed so hard because she found the question hilarious! She answered by saying that at 19 years old, she still lived at home with her parents and her parents had never exposed her to debt. The concept of debt was so foreign to her that she found it hard to believe or even imagine using her hard-earned money from a major title win to pay off debt. She is blessed to have such financially disciplined parents.

That should be our attitude toward debt. Do not become enslaved to lenders just because you want to have a house in your name. Whichever way you slice and dice it, when you owe someone else money, they have a huge upper hand over you.

The Power of Delayed Gratification

Do not make purchases on impulse, expensive purchases especially. Sleep on the decision. If after a day or two you still really want the item, then go ahead and buy it. But make sure you can truly afford it (remember, no debt!).

Also, make the shift from having a consumer mindset. The idea of always buying will leave you broke and keep you poor. Instead, start to think about ways to create, invent, and produce. Those are the actions that produce excellence.

Like many of you reading this, I like the fine things of life. I love fashion and like to dress nicely. However, I am also very debt averse. I sell or donate items I no longer need on an ongoing basis. The earnings I get from selling those items are what I use to buy the items I want.

I now make it a point to buy timeless, classic clothing pieces and accessories. They last longer and have a good resale value; I get my money's worth from them. I do not shy away from scouring consignment stores to buy items that I want in great, preloved condition.

I share this to let you know that you can still have the nice things of life by being patient and employing strategies that help to ensure you are spending within your means.

Here's another thing to ask when considering a purchase: Does it spark joy in your life?

I learned to ask this question from organization and life-style expert Marie Kondo. She advises that we get rid of items that no longer spark joy in our lives, either through selling or donating them. So why not get into the habit of donating or selling items you no longer need when you acquire new ones? This will help to keep clutter at bay, and keeping your space clutter free has a multitude of benefits that include promoting mental well-being.

One last piece of advice: Before you go buy something new, first "shop your home." You will be very surprised at what you may end up finding. Most of us have way too many items to begin with, and we tend to forget what's tucked away in various corners of the house.

Final Words of Advice

I hope you consider the financial concepts discussed in this chapter. They are universal best practices that have been shown time and again to produce great results in the quest for personal excellence.

The idea is not just to live and enjoy life, but to live and enjoy life purposefully. It is important to start to look at our financial habits critically to see if they are impeding us or helping us to grow in our pursuit of excellence.

This is not a condemnation epistle but a battle cry to do better with our finances. Ask yourself this question: Why should you be trusted with more money, if you are unable to properly manage the finances at your disposal now?

One last thought. Anyone can choose to make foolish decisions with their finances. But now that your mindset is renewed and you know better, the responsibility to do better with your finances lies on you. Please do not use your hard-earned money to perpetuate financial foolishness. Make the decision to be guided by financial wisdom going forward.

KEY POINTS

◎   A person has no business desiring to own or handle plenty of money if the desire to learn how to master financial excellence is not there.

◎   Spending more than you earn is very unwise. When we spend more than we earn, we are living beyond our means.

◎ A budget is necessary to help you accurately identify your monthly expenses and to ensure that those expenses are way below your monthly income.

◎ Having an emergency fund will help to ensure you are well prepared for life's emergencies.

◎ Buying with a credit card is spending money that does not belong to you. If you cannot afford what you are trying to purchase with your available cash, then you simply cannot afford it—plain and simple.

◎ When you owe, you are bound to the lender in many more ways than you may realize.

◎ The idea of always needing to buy things will leave you broke and keep you poor. Instead, start to think about ways to create, invent, and produce.

◎ Before you go buy something new, shop your home—you will be very surprised at what you may end up finding. Most of us have way too many items.

◎ It is important to start to look at our financial habits critically to see if they are impeding us or helping us to grow in personal excellence.

TAKE ACTION

◎ Use your imagination to visualize where you would like to be financially. Be audacious.

◎ Write down the vision imagined for your financial future in a journal.

◎ Take it a step further and represent the vision with concrete images and put it on a vision board.

◎ Put the vision board in a prominent place so it serves as a constant reminder of the goals you wish to achieve.

◎ If your vision is to get out of debt, have that goal in front of you so that you can direct any extra money you get toward paying down your debt.

◎ Now come up with a system or process to turn your vision into reality. A vision board or visualization alone will not suffice.

◎ There are additional steps you can take now to get out of debt. Are you paying too much for your cell phone and other services? Take the time to write down the different amounts you pay for each bill. See if you are able to switch to a cheaper plan or even switch service providers altogether to save on how much you are paying. This involves some work, but it will be so worth it in the long run. Tackle one bill at a time.

◎ If you are spending more than you make or living paycheck to paycheck, stop immediately and come up with a better plan. Live well below your means.

Doing so will probably require cutting out a lot of unnecessary spending after carrying out an honest evaluation of your finances. Sacrifices and delayed gratification will help you tremendously.

◎ Set up a budget today. Due your research online to find what budget system works best for you. A budget is the only way to determine how much you have and what is available to spend each month.

◎ Get into the habit of saving and investing.

◎ Invest for the long term. Watch documentaries and read books on long-term investing so you can make good decisions that work for you. There is ample free information out there on the subject.

◎ You are responsible for learning and doing all that is necessary to get out of debt. You also owe it to yourself to learn and grow in financial excellence.

CHAPTER 12

EXCELLENCE PRINCIPLE 11:
Speak with Intention and Purpose

THERE IS NO SUCH thing as "mere" words. Our words carry tremendous power. As a result, we cannot afford to be careless with our words. The words we speak daily can make or break, heal or wound, build or tear down . . . and the list goes on. Whenever we are mindful to consider the purpose and intention behind the words we are about to utter and use our words wisely, we are operating and speaking from a place of excellence.

We have the power to use our words to transform the world around us. Just ponder for a moment on the power and impact of kind words spoken to another person. A kind word spoken to a stranger has the power to truly make their day and transform their life for the better. We can use our words to boost a person's confidence and even give hope. Conversely, unkind words spoken to a person can ruin the person's entire day and make them feel totally worthless.

In a 2008 neuroscience study entitled "Do words hurt? Brain activation during the processing of pain-related words," authors Maria Richter, et al, revealed and proved that negative words release stress and anxiety-inducing hormones in subjects.[9]

Dr. Masaru Emoto, a scientist from Japan, did groundbreaking work on the effect of words on water.[10] In his study, he was able to show how kind and unkind words affect the molecular structure of water.

Dr. Masaru Emoto showed that water carries information in it. He froze water on petri dishes at -25 C. for three hours and viewed it under a powerful microscope. He discovered that when water is exposed to negative words and thoughts, it forms ugly crystals or no crystals at all. On the contrary, when water is exposed to positive words, positive prayers, and music, it forms beautiful symmetrical crystal shapes. Dr. Emoto stated that "God put this hidden message in water to let us know that everything in the universe should be created harmoniously and in unity."

Dr. Emoto noted that the tone of words spoken also affected the structure of the crystals. Words spoken harshly to the water-filled petri dish led to the formation of ugly looking crystals, or none at all. Words spoken lovingly to water in the petri dish led to the formation of beautiful crystals.

The findings from Dr. Emoto's research are significant because water makes up roughly 65 percent of the human body. The human brain alone consists of approximately 80 percent water. Just imagine what happens on our inside when we are constantly exposed to negative news, or when we engage in self-deprecating thoughts all day long? It affects the harmonious state of our body.

Self-talk, either negative or positive, sends vibrations (good or toxic) all over our body.

Cognitive neuroscientist Dr. Caroline Leaf has shown that toxic thoughts are actual real things in the mind that travel throughout the nervous system.[11] We cannot have a mind filled with toxic thoughts and expect to have a positive life. This is because we manifest our thoughts through our behavior and our words. What is internal becomes external, affecting the world around us.

How many times a day do we use words carelessly? We say things like "I hate my hair," "I'm so stupid," "I'm such a klutz." We never think that these words bring negative energy into our vibration and affect us on a physical level—but they do.

Emoto's experiments were conducted with water. Why? Because sound vibration travels through water four times faster than it does through open air. This helps us to see and understand how quickly the vibration from negative words resonates in our cells.

In a different experiment, Dr. Emoto had rice covered with water in three different dishes. For one month, he spoke kind words to the rice in dish one, unkind words such as "You are an idiot" to the rice in dish two, and said nothing at all to the water-covered rice in dish three. After one month, the rice in dish one started to ferment and give off a pleasant aroma; the rice in dish two turned black; and the rice in dish three turned black.[12]

Dr. Emoto used this experiment to illustrate how words affect children. This is important because children require a lot of positive attention to thrive. They need to be spoken to in a kind and loving manner regularly.

Award-winning speaker Josephine Lee, in her Ted Talk "The Power of Transformative Words," shared about a time when she volunteered at a maximum juvenile delinquency center's study hall, where she assisted the inmates with homework. When she switched to addressing the inmates as gentlemen, instead of "Guys" or" Hey, you," it gave them a deep sense of dignity and honor. They paid attention in study hall, sat up straight, and were more inviting and open to learning from her.

Our words, or even the tone we choose to use with our words, can change everything. Our words carry the power of life and death. As a result, there are consequences to the words we utter, whether those words are aimed at others or internally at ourselves. We can use them to heal or divide. Or we can use them to hurt or heal. A person of excellence is always mindful of this.

How to Use Your Words to Build

Affirmations

Affirmations are positive statements that we say to ourselves. They are intended to provide encouragement, emotional support, or motivation, and can be an effective tool for self-improvement and positive thinking. If you find that your internal conversation is filled with toxicity or is undermining who you are in any way, stop immediately and switch your internal conversation to positive affirmations about yourself.

Carry a set of positive affirmation cards with you or have it stored on your phone. Read the cards back to yourself so often that you eventually have them memorized. This is the weapon from your arsenal that you pull out whenever those deceitful negative voices start. This is how you silence those contradictory voices.

Here is a list of a few of my favorite affirmations. You are welcome to adopt them as yours.

◎ I am valuable. I add great value to the world, wherever I go.
◎ I enhance and complement every life I come across.

- ◎ I am the light of the world. A city on a hill that cannot be hidden.
- ◎ I am deeply and truly loved.
- ◎ I am a beautiful person on the inside and on the outside.
- ◎ I am confident, bold, and strong.
- ◎ I love people like my heavenly Father loves people.
- ◎ I am unique, awesomely and wonderfully made.
- ◎ I am God's most amazing workmanship. All of me, every part, is wonderfully made.
- ◎ I am God's masterpiece.
- ◎ I live a life of abundance.
- ◎ My needs are met with plenty left over to be a blessing to others.
- ◎ I will fulfill to the very last letter my purpose on this planet.
- ◎ I am distinguished and preferred because an EXCELLENT spirit is within me.
- ◎ I am a person of excellence and integrity. Every day I strive to be better in every area of my life.
- ◎ I am healthy and strong. I eat right and exercise regularly.
- ◎ Today I choose to stay full of peace, hope, joy, and expectancy.
- ◎ I will flourish in every area of my life, including my relationships, career, business, health, and finances.
- ◎ I love all people and have a deep love for all of humanity.
- ◎ The days and years ahead shall be so much better than the former.
- ◎ My presence lights up rooms and brightens lives.
- ◎ I am God's masterpiece, created in His image. I am extraordinary!
- ◎ It is my time to shine and step into the open doors and new levels of opportunity that God has in store.

- ◎ Great blessings and great opportunities are coming my way today/this week/this month/this year.
- ◎ I am uniquely gifted and I always do excellent work.
- ◎ Men and women of eminence will notice my work. I will stand before kings.

Save these affirmations. Print them, do what you wish with them. Counter those pesky negative thoughts with them whenever they show up.

Affirmations are indeed powerful. I encourage you to add the recital of uplifting encouraging affirmations to your daily routine. When circumstances and life try to pull us down, affirmations remind us of who we truly are.

Reframe Your Thoughts Around the Words You Speak

Do not use your words to take ownership of things you do not want in your life. For instance, it is okay to acknowledge a cancer diagnosis. But taking ownership of that which you do not want in the first place by repeatedly saying "my cancer" every time you talk about your diagnosis is not exactly helping the situation. By attaching "my" to the diagnosis, you are taking ownership of that which you do not want. Remember, our words carry power.

Instead of *my* cancer, refer to it as "the cancer diagnosis." This detaches *you* from the cancer. I've heard stories of people who know how powerful words are who choose not to even call out their diagnosis. You decide on what is best for you. But the point is not to claim ownership of that which you do not want in the first place by going around saying *my* cancer, *my* sinuses,

146

my cold, *my* asthma. Find a way of rephrasing your sentences so you are acknowledging the diagnosis that you have but do not take ownership of it.

Here are examples of statements I make whenever I feel under the weather: "I am fighting flu symptoms." "I have been battling flu-like symptoms all weekend long and need to rest as a result." Those statements have a more proactive and positive ring to them. I am not in denial of how I am feeling. But I am not just passively accepting the illness either.

I will take it a step further by saying, don't focus so much on what you do not want in the first place by talking about and discussing it all the time. Whatever it is that we choose to focus on—particularly when that focus comes in the forms of words—becomes magnified over time.

Instead, keep your thoughts continually fixed on all that is authentic and real, honorable and admirable, beautiful and respectful, pure and holy, merciful and kind.

Several years ago I worked with a client named Linda. In our very first session, which was by phone, it wasn't even up to ten minutes into our discussion when I noticed that her every other sentence was laced with either a negative complaint or just something negative in general. Nothing was right about the world or her life, as far as Linda was concerned. This incessant negativity was a long-standing bad habit that Linda did not even realize she had. She said things like "It's just too much"; "I'm tired"; "I'm just exhausted"; "I can't do that"; and "I feel like I need a vacation every week." I found it very puzzling and in fact draining just listening to her as she spoke.

My next session with Linda happened to be in person. I arrived at our meeting place several minutes before she did. As Linda walked toward me, I saw that she walked like she talked. Linda carried herself as though she had all of the weight of the world on her shoulders. She walked as though she was literally dragging herself though life. Her shoulders were slumped and she looked like she was indeed exhausted. Unknown to Linda, the negative words she spoke day in and day out had now become a self-fulfilling prophecy. She had had this internal conversation about always being tired and overwhelmed with all the different things she had to do daily so many times that it was now part of her identity, and it now reflected in her demeanor and how she carried herself.

In our second session, I pointed this out to Linda, and as expected, she did not even realize that it was a problem or habit. So we started addressing this behavior. We worked on creating a list of affirmations for her to use to first change her internal conversations to positive ones. The list of affirmations was also used to remind Linda that it was not okay to go around all day long thinking "I'm tired" or "I'm exhausted."

Linda also had to change her outlook on life. Instead of seeing the glass half empty at all times, which sooner than later would make one start to feel and look tired and exhausted, which is what had happened to Linda, a more positive approach was seeing the glass half full. I explained to her how this perspective on life will help to foster positive thoughts and words and possible solutions to issues and problems she faces in life.

We also critically looked at Linda's daily schedule and routine and discussed ways to change the stressors that led to her feeling like she was exhausted all the time.

After only a few weeks of working with Linda, good changes began to happen. Linda worked hard to strengthen her new habit of reminding herself with positive affirmations of who she truly was: beautiful, strong, poised, and confident, to name a few. As she continued to diligently change her internal narrative, Linda started to look like a totally different person physically. She had lost some weight and now walked with poise and confidence.

Linda was happy with the results and changes she was beginning to see in her life. Yes, she did not realize initially that she was using her very own words to suck the life out of herself. But now that she knew better, she was able to channel the power and energy of her words into infusing life and positivity into her life and situations.

What's in Your Heart?

Whenever we speak, we do so out of the abundance of what is stored up in our hearts. The gateway to our heart is our eyes, ears, and environment. So what we watch and listen to, and those we spend the most time around, all affect what we say. Our words are shaped by what we see, what we hear, our environment, and more.

The true state of a person's heart is revealed through their words. Have you ever met or known someone who when they speak, they speak from a place of bitterness or resentment? It is almost as though every sentence is laced with a splash of bitterness here and a pinch of resentment there. Sadly, that is exactly what happens when toxic thoughts go unchecked. They take root in the heart and sprout through spoken words and actions. Our words, the words we speak daily, have a way of revealing the true state of our heart. Guard your heart against toxicity, such as offenses, bitterness, and the like, so that your words do not betray you.

Your Word Is Your Bond

If you say that you are going to do something, simply do it. Sadly, we now live in a day and age where people's words often do not hold water. The words they utter often lack credibility or even validity.

It shows how little value people place on words in today's society. Be the exception. You are a person of excellence. Choose to be different when it comes to your words.

Not too long ago, I sent out invites for my youngest son's birthday celebration. I requested that the parents RSVP so I could plan accordingly. One of the parents emailed back to say she would be there. I saw her a few days later and she gushed about how excited her daughter was about coming to Isaiah's birthday party. She also reconfirmed that they would both be there. Well, she did not show up on the day of the event. She also did not bother to send any messages or call. She just simply chose not to bring her child. I happened to see her the next day and it was not until I mentioned I did not see her and her daughter at the celebration that she casually mentioned something along the lines of "Oh, she was tired so we couldn't come." She expressed no remorse. To her it was apparently just normal to say she would do something and then turn around the next moment and decide not to do it. That speaks volumes about that person because how we do one thing is usually reflective of how we do most things.

Excellence is saying you are going to do something and then following through. It is better for you not to commit in the first place, instead of committing and then not following through. If due to extenuating circumstances you have to break your promise, then be quick to inform the stakeholders. Let them know about the new development as soon as you are able to so they can make the necessary changes or updates.

Keep Your Words Gentle and Soft

It's been said that *how* we say something is even more important than what we say. The tone with which we talk matters greatly. You can diffuse a heated discourse with softly spoken words. Or add more fuel to a heated conversation with an aggressive, challenging tone.

We all get angry. Anger is a real and valid emotion. But we do not need to give full vent to our anger by saying what is on our mind right there and there. When emotions are raging, it is wise to bite the tongue, walk away from the situation, and come back to it when the emotions are more stable. Words stick and are remembered for a long, long time. Words carry a lot of weight and should be used with wisdom and caution.

Use your words to speak things of excellence into your life. Remember that your words carry power. Use the power of your spoken words wisely and positively.

KEY POINTS

◎ We have the power to use our words to transform the world around us.

◎ Negative words spoken to others or that we speak to ourselves via unchecked toxic thoughts release stress- and anxiety-inducing hormones.

◎ Self-talk, either negative or positive, sends vibrations (good or toxic) all over our body.

◎ Children require a lot of positive attention to thrive. They need to be spoken to in a kind and loving manner regularly.

◎ When circumstances and life try to pull us down, affirmations remind us of who we truly are.

◎ Do not use your words to take ownership of things you do not want in your life.

◎ Our words are shaped by what we see and hear, by the people in our environment, and more.

◎ The true state of a person's heart is revealed through their words.

◎ Excellence is saying you are going to do something and then following through.

◎ *How* we say something is even more important than what we say. The tone with which we speak matters greatly.

TAKE ACTION

Take inventory of your daily internal conversations.

Now ask yourself, are you using your words to build yourself up or tear yourself down? Do you subconsciously call yourself self-defeating names? Do you say things like "I'm so slow" or "I suck when it comes to directions"? If so, change your conversation. Use words that reflect what you want to be true about yourself. Rephrase that which you have always said negatively about yourself in a positive light. From today, start to use your words to build yourself up and not tear yourself down.

And what about the people in your life? Do you speak negative words about loved ones or your situations? Do you say things like "We are always broke in this house" or "My kids are nutzos"?

Our words sooner than later become self-fulfilling prophecies. That is why they are so powerful. For example, if you say to yourself enough times, "I suck when it comes to driving directions," you might not even bother trying to get better at driving directions, which will inadvertently lead to you becoming or remaining truly poor at understanding driving directions.

Instead, change your personal narrative about yourself. And change the limiting, long-standing narratives that you have had about your loved ones. Use your words to generate higher expectations for yourself, your loved ones, and the situations which confront you. Doing so will then in effect lead to higher performance and better outcomes. Use your words to speak life, hope, and power over your situations and over yourself.

Let your words define the story of who you are, and let it be a good story.

CHAPTER 13

EXCELLENCE PRINCIPLE 12:
You Become What You Eat

NONE OF WHAT YOU have read so far in this book matters much if your main challenge is simply mustering the strength to make it through each day due to poor health. Many of us have neglected our bodies through making poor diet choices over the years, which have now resulted in poor health conditions. These poor health conditions, which may include chronic illnesses, sabotage our potential for living a life of excellence.

It is indeed true that "health is wealth." We need a healthy, functioning vessel (body) to pursue our dreams and fulfill the purpose and vision for our lives.

By the time this book is published, I will still be in my mid-forties, and I am in great health. I do not suffer from any chronic disease, nor do I have any underlying health problems. However, this did not happen by chance. I have had to make many changes over the years that have led me to where I am today. Read on to hear about those changes.

Here's the main thing you must accept: There is no shortcut to great health. Great health is created and maintained by consistent, mindful actions. It may seem like you are getting away with eating junk food all the time, and you may feel invincible as a result. Newsflash: You are not! The human body is great at keeping records and taking notes. Sooner than later, those poor diet choices will catch up with you. The resulting effects are always unpleasant and sadly sometimes long-lasting. This is why we have to be intentional about cultivating food habits that promote good health and excellence.

In our society today, overly processed foods that have little to no nutritional value are what you will find on most of the store shelves. Aside from having little to no nutritional value, these overly processed foods have been linked to cancer, chronic diseases, and more.

Rethink Your Diet

The first place to start when revamping your health is with the food you consume daily. I do not mean eating less of what you are already eating now. After all, those foods may be the main reason behind the health issues you are facing in the first place. Revamping your health may require changing your diet completely. A complete overhaul may be what is required.

In my opinion, food is to be enjoyed and also to be seen as a catalyst for the healing, growth, and repair of the cells and organs in our body. A person cannot overload their body with foods with little to no nutritional value and somehow expect their body to function optimally and support their goal to live a life of excellence. Food is fuel for the body. Just as you cannot put adulterated fuel or contaminated low-grade gasoline in your car and somehow expect your car to run flawlessly, you cannot expect your mind and body to function optimally on poor quality food. No, that is not going to happen. As a matter of fact, just as the car's engine will in no time break down, so will your precious human body. If you abuse it long enough, it will eventually break down beyond repair.

Before it gets to that, make healthy choices now that will do your body good, not harm. Here are a few of the steps I took toward revamping and taking charge of my health:

Gut Health

I took control of my gut health. I suffered from bloating, cramps, constipation, and extreme fatigue for years. I did test after test, and my doctor prescribed roughly fifteen different supplements to combat the issues—but that did not work. My primary physician thought maybe it was Lupus at one point. Test after test proved that was not the root cause of my symptoms. It was not until I started to do my own research that I discovered that an unhealthy gut biome (the community of microorganisms, including bacteria, yeast, and fungi, that live in the digestive tract) may be the root of the problem. The gut biome is known to have a major influence on health, metabolism, body weight, the immune system, appetite, mood digestion, and more. So you can just imagine what happens when your gut biome is out of whack. I decided to reboot my gut health, the same way you would a computer.

- ◎ I eliminated sugar from my diet for a long period of time, about five months. I have drastically cut down my intake of sugar since.
- ◎ I eliminated inflammatory foods like seed oils. These oils are readily available on supermarket shelves in the

form of corn oil, canola oil, and the like. They are heavily processed compared to other oils, like olive oil.

◎ I stopped using spices with artificial ingredients in my food. For example, I no longer cook with seasoning cubes because they are loaded with concentrated preservatives and artificial ingredients. I now use only natural herbs and whole spices when I cook. My dishes have never been more flavorful, by the way!

◎ I eliminated shelf-stable foods from my diet.

◎ I mastered how to read nutritional information on foods and also identify the misleading and confusing information that is found on a lot of food labels. I urge you to learn how to understand food labels and familiarize yourself with the different ingredients so you know what is off limits.

◎ I increased my intake of water. I now drink over 100 ounces of water per day.

◎ I started to exercise regularly, four to five times a week.

I replaced the inflammatory foods mentioned above with whole natural foods that are good for my gut health. Some of those foods include fermented foods, salads, and other various kinds of food made from natural ingredients that have been minimally processed. The oils that I use in cooking are now all cold-pressed oils with high smoke points, and I keep oil usage to a minimum.

It took approximately five months to revamp my gut health, but the results have been outstanding:

◎ All of the previously mentioned symptoms are gone. They literally disappeared one after the other as I switched out my diet.

- ◎ I have also thankfully remained free of any underlying health conditions.
- ◎ I now take only five supplements on average, a major drop from the fifteen that I used to have to take.
- ◎ My strength has increased tremendously.
- ◎ The extreme fatigue is gone.

My lab numbers have remained excellent year after year. My primary physician never fails to tell me how amazed he is at the turnaround in my health whenever I go in for my annual checkup.

Now, when it comes to my health and that of my family, I am very proactive. As a family, we stay on the offense by building up our immune systems through making wise choices about the foods we consume. I now eat mostly foods that help to keep my gut biome thriving.

You cannot put a price on great health. You are better off paying the price of being disciplined in your eating habits now and reaping the many great benefits of doing so now and in the future.

Do all of the steps and strategies I have highlighted make you totally invincible to sickness and disease? No! However, fueling your body with what it needs to function as it was designed has proven to be the better option in so many ways. Certainly it is much superior to eating junk food and having to deal with the detrimental consequences which may result, including possible premature death.

Beware of Detrimental Chemicals and Additives

Before moving to the United States in 2001, I lived in the United Kingdom for a number of years. I experienced major culture shock, especially when it came to food, when I started living in the United States. Europe is also known to have stricter food regulations than the United States. There are many ingredients banned in many European countries that are still added to our foods here in the United States.

For example, in the US, manufacturers use potassium bromate in bread products to strengthen the dough and make it rise higher. The International Agency for Research on Cancer classes this additive as a 2B carcinogen, which means that it's "possibly carcinogenic to humans." It is banned in many places, including the European Union, my country of birth Nigeria, South Korea, India, Argentina, and China.

The US has much weaker standards when it comes to pesticide residues in food. A recent report from Pesticide Action Network UK gives this example: In the US, grapes can be sold with 1,000 times more propargite than is legal in the UK. According to the EPA, this chemical can cause skin and eye irritation and is a "probable human carcinogen."

Some studies show that the food coloring yellow 6 (also called sunset yellow FCF) "may have an adverse effect on activity and attention in children." In the EU, this is acknowledged on labels for products that contain this food coloring.

In 2022, the EU banned a food colorant called titanium dioxide. The move came after studies showed that it might damage DNA. This same food colorant is still approved for use in the U.S.

When it comes to food additives and ingredients that are deemed potentially risky, the EU takes a precautionary approach. They ban or add warning labels to these additives for their citizens. The US takes a reactive approach. It does not remove additives from the food supply chain until they have been proven dangerous, which can take a very long time and a lot of red tape.

When my oldest son was born, I chose the traditional route of nursing and supplementing with baby formula. At around three months old, Caleb started to break out in hives, amongst other things. It was clear that he was reacting to something, we just did not know what it was at the time. We tried different things, but the skin condition was persistent and worsened to the point that he was prescribed topical steroids by his pediatrician. Coupled with all of that, he also developed upper respiratory problems that landed us in the hospital emergency room many times.

I kept trying different body lotions and kept switching baby formulas, but nothing seemed to work. The issues continue for about a year. The symptoms would at times subside for a week or two, and then out of nowhere flare up again. After trying everything, one day I took a wild guess that maybe the food he was eating was the culprit. We weaned him off the particular baby formula he was on at the time. In just a few weeks, all of the conditions disappeared. I should add that a lot of prayers went into the mix as well.

When I was pregnant with my second child , I started to do a lot more research on the ingredients of baby formula. I was shocked at some of my findings. The ingredients baby formula is made from are downright scary. Some have no place in the human body. Baby formula for my second child was sourced from Europe. I found a brand with very clean organic ingredients. Thankfully I was able to breastfeed as well.

As of today, none of my kids have allergies or any health conditions. Caleb's skin condition and upper respiratory issues have disappeared and there has not been any recurrence in over fifteen years.

Portion Control Matters

The food portions served in restaurants in the UK and many other European countries are much smaller than what you will get in an average American restaurant. When I relocated to the United States in 2001, I was shocked at the large food portions served in restaurants. In comparison to the UK, the portions in some of the restaurants are enough for four people.

Eating half the portion and saving the rest for later is eating only half the calories in one sitting. The other half can be saved for dinner or even the next day. Portion control has played a huge role in helping me to keep my weight stable over the years.

Supplements

The human body is so complex that minerals and vitamins have to be at optimal levels for it to function well. We used to be able to get all of the vitamins and minerals our body needs to function well from food, but not anymore. The soil has been highly depleted of the majority of its rich minerals and vitamins, making it necessary to take supplements.

As mentioned previously, I take several supplements daily. Getting blood work done at your doctor's office will reveal any deficiencies in minerals and vitamins that need to be rectified by supplements or other interventions. Ask your primary physician to carry out the relevant tests to determine if you are lacking in any necessary vitamins or minerals. Based on the results, they will then tell you what to do to remedy the situation. But you have to ask. Make it a point to ask at your next doctor's visit. I found out I was iron deficient a few years back via a routine test carried out by my doctor, and I was able to quickly correct that with the proper dosage of iron he prescribed.

Drink Water

Drink lots of it! The human body is 70 percent water. We need water to move much-needed nutrients around the body and waste matter out of it. The blood is made of water, and cannot supply the organs with all they need to function optimally if you are not drinking enough water. View water as a vehicle that transports to the different organs in your body what they need to function. Water is also the sole vehicle that is used to flush out waste, toxins, and the residue from the different organs and cells.

I try to drink at least 100 ounces of water daily. I'm usually very thirsty after exercising, so I seize the opportunity to consume 30 to 50 ounces of water as soon as I leave the gym. Then I continue to drink water throughout the day.

I have heard a lot of people say they do not like the taste of water, so they drink flavored water. Again, know what you are consuming. What is the water flavored with? Studies have shown that the term "natural flavoring" is an ambiguous label that food makers are allowed to slap on drinks and foods without exactly disclosing what the "natural" flavors consist of. Be cautious, because the term "natural flavor" can be misleading as it does not necessarily mean that the flavor is 100 percent natural. In the United States, for example, the Food and Drug Administration allows natural flavors to contain synthetic solvents and preservatives.

But there are plenty of healthy workarounds. You can make your own flavored seltzer water by simply adding fruits to it. It's delicious.

Sleep and Proper Rest

Our body requires sleep and rest to recalibrate. Make sure you are getting ample sleep daily. Yes, there are times when it is necessary to burn the midnight candle. But those times should be few and far in between. Again, your body cannot optimally function without proper sleep. It is not designed that way.

Just like a small child gets highly irritable when he/she has not had enough sleep, studies have shown that lack of sleep is highly detrimental to our physical and mental well-being. Lack of sleep can affect your immune system. Studies show that people who do not get quality sleep or enough sleep are more susceptible to viral infections such as the common cold virus. Lack of sleep can also affect how fast you recover if you do get sick. Long-term lack of sleep also increases your risk of obesity, diabetes, and heart and blood vessel (cardiovascular) disease.

Other studies show that lack of sleep and having poor quality sleep affect both how we feel and how we function. These conditions are associated with:

- excess body weight and obesity
- type 2 diabetes
- cardiovascular disease
- depression
- anxiety
- impaired cognitive function.

Irritability and mood disorders can also result from poor sleep. Chronic sleep problems have been linked to depression, anxiety, and mental distress. For example, one study reported that participants who slept only 4.5 hours per night were more stressed, sad, angry, and mentally exhausted than a comparison group that enjoyed longer sleep.[13]

One final note: Teens, tweens, and young adults are notorious for having poor sleeping habits. The reason your young adult is always so irritable and moody may be because they are not getting good quality sleep. Check on your young ones. Help them to adopt good sleep habits for their own good.

Exercise

It has been said that movement is life! The basic truth is this. In order for your muscles not to atrophy, you have to keep them moving. It is the basic principle of "You will lose what you do not use."

At the barest minimum, stretch. I'm in my mid-forties. The truth is now I need to stretch out the various muscle groups in my body daily in order for them to work as they are designed to. I do most of my stretching when I first wake up in the morning and it makes a world of difference.

A sedentary lifestyle is harmful in so many ways. The human body was not designed to sit in one position for long hours on end. This leads to injury, amongst other things. My many years of sitting in front of a computer, for sometimes eight hours straight, when I worked in corporate America eventually caught up with me. It took a long time to heal from lower back pain.

Weak muscles in any part of the body, by the way, will lead to a host of other secondary related issues. A study published in the *BMC Public Health* journal found that physical activity and exercise reduce mortality rates and improve quality of life with minimal or no safety concerns. The study also concluded that a sedentary lifestyle is a major risk factor for noncommunicable diseases such as cardiovascular diseases, cancer, and diabetes.[14]

It has been estimated that approximately 3.2 million deaths each year are attributable to insufficient levels of physical activity.

Research has shown that exercise has many benefits. It can help prevent and improve health problems such as high blood pressure, diabetes, arthritis, heart disease, stroke, high cholesterol, type 2 diabetes, osteoporosis, and loss of muscle mass. Exercise can also improve mood and reduce anxiety, depression, and ADHD. It can relieve stress, improve memory, and boost overall mood.

Exercise can help with weight loss and better weight management. It provides an energy boost, better posture, stronger bones, and better looking skin and complexion. Exercise makes everyday tasks easier and improves sleep quality.

Your Skin

The skin is the largest organ of the body. If your skin is experiencing discomfort or irritation, what you put on your skin could be the culprit. In recent years I have swapped out soaps laden with artificial ingredients with organic handmade soaps made of natural ingredients. That has practically removed all incidents of skin irritation from my life.

I now make my own body lotion from shea butter sourced from West Africa, mixing it with essential oils and other natural ingredients. On the rare occasion that I buy skin butter or lotion, I buy from companies that make lotions from clean ingredients.

Final Thoughts

After reading this chapter and learning my personal health-care habits, you may think, "Wow! That's a lot of work." I can appreciate that response. But my answer is that I understand that I cannot live a life of excellence or pursue my life's goals if I feed my body with foods and things that are detrimental to its optimal functioning. I want to live a life of excellence.

In this chapter I have shared habits and health strategies that have worked for me because I want *you* to be in great health. You need to be in order to pursue excellence in your life. I hope my suggestions are helpful and lead you down fruitful paths. But keep in mind that you will need to find out what works for you, and this may differ in some ways from what works for me, or any other person.

I believe that excellence will be unachievable if a person continues to make poor choices when it comes to their diet and health, as they have to deal with and live with the consequences. At best, let this chapter jump-start the process of your learning about how what you consume and how you sleep and exercise affects you. Ask questions of your doctor at your next visit and make those necessary simple changes that can lead to huge improvements in your overall health.

My prayer, hope, and desire for you as you read and apply the principles outlined in this book is this: "Dear friend, I pray that you may enjoy good health and that all may go well with you, even as your soul is getting along well."—3 John 1:2

KEY POINTS

◎ We need a healthy, functioning vessel (body) to live a life of excellence and fulfill the purpose and vision for our lives.

◎ There is no shortcut to great health.

◎ A person cannot overload their body with foods with little to no nutritional value and somehow expect their body to function excellently. The exact opposite is what will happen.

◎ The gut biome is known to have a major influence on health, metabolism, body weight, the immune system, appetite, mood, digestion, and more.

◎ We used to be able to get all of the vitamins and minerals our body needs to function well from food, but not anymore, hence why we need to take appropriate supplements.

◎ We need to drink enough water to move much-needed nutrients around the body and waste matter out of it.

◎ Studies show that people who do not get quality sleep or enough sleep are more susceptible to viral infections such as the common cold virus.

◎ Scientific studies show that long-term lack of sleep also increases your risk of obesity, diabetes, and heart and blood vessel (cardiovascular) disease.

◎ In order for your muscles not to atrophy, you have to keep them moving via exercise. Weak muscles in any part of the body also lead to a host of related secondary issues.

◎ A sedentary lifestyle is a major risk factor for non-communicable diseases such as cardiovascular diseases, cancer, and diabetes.

TAKE ACTION

Evaluate your current diet and eating habits. Are they helping you toward your goal of achieving excellence in your life or are they impeding you? Be truthful and honest with yourself.

Use the information outlined in this chapter to make the needed changes. Start by taking baby steps. Think about how you can make healthier choices in different areas of your life to help you excel in energy and well-being.

Remember that the information I have outlined is not all-inclusive. It is to help you jump-start the process of becoming your own health advocate, and taking a proactive approach when it comes to your health.

Learn and master how to read food labels. Know the difference between misleading and true information when it comes to listed ingredients. Eliminate or greatly reduce your intake of highly processed shelf-stable foods.

I like and subscribe to the idea of getting most of my foods from the outer perimeter of the grocery store. That's where most perishable and healthier food options are found.

The shelf-stable foods are found mostly in the aisle sections of the supermarket.

Build up your gut biome. Feed it with foods that are good for it.

At your next doctor's visit, ask that they check to see if you are deficient in vitamins and minerals. If a deficiency is identified, remedy it before it leads to other issues.

Become your own health advocate.

CHAPTER 14

EXCELLENCE PRINCIPLE 13:
We All Need to Rest

REST AND EXCELLENCE ARE not mutually exclusive, but rather complementary. Rest is an essential component of working well and working smart, as it helps us to recharge our energy and our minds, consolidate our memories, and enhance our creativity. Many researchers and creative thinkers have found that resting more boosts their productivity and performance, as well as their well-being.

In his book *Rest: Why You Get More Done When You Work Less*, Alex Soojung-Kim Pang explores the common thread that ties together work, rest, and creativity.[15] He shares findings from studies carried out on some of the world's most accomplished and influential figures, among them Charles Darwin, the British naturalist who proposed the theory of biological evolution by natural selection; Charles Dickens, the famous English novelist who wrote several of my favorite classic novels of all time, such as *Oliver Twist, A Tale of Two Cities, Great Expectations,* and *A Christmas Carol*; Henri Poincaré, the French mathematician, physicist, and philosopher who is considered one of the founders of modern mathematics and one of the greatest thinkers of all time; and Ingmar Bergman, the Swedish screenwriter, film, and theater director who is widely considered one of the greatest and most influential film directors of our time.

Charles Darwin's work days consisted of three intense ninety-minute periods. In between those periods he napped, went for walks, and did other things.

Henri Poincaré kept very regular hours. He did his hardest thinking between 10 a.m. and noon, and again between 5 and 7 in the afternoon. In short, this nineteenth century mathematical genius worked just enough to get his mind around a problem—about four hours a day.

Charles Dickens wrote for about five hours a day, from 9 a.m. to 2 p.m., after which he would go for long walks and relax.[16]

Pang relates how the studies reveal that these men did not work for endless long hours on end. They only spent a few hours a day doing important work. The rest of the time they were hiking mountains, taking naps, going on walks with friends, or just sitting and thinking. Their creative achievements and productivity resulted from only a few hours of concentrated work at a time, supported by plenty of rest and leisure.

Another study focused on violin students at a conservatory in Berlin in the 1980s. Researchers Ericsson, Krampe, and Tesch-Römer were interested in what sets outstanding students apart from merely good ones.[17] They found that the great violin students did not just practice more than the average, they practiced more deliberately. Deliberate practice in any skill or field requires focused attention and a specific goal of improving performance, with the purpose of achieving mastery and excellence.

The best students generally followed a pattern of practicing hardest and longest in the morning, taking a nap in the afternoon, and then having a second practice. The outstanding students figured out early that rest is important, and that some of our most creative work happens when we take the kinds of breaks that allow our unconscious mind to keep plugging away.

Science also demonstrates that the body as an information system always rebuilds and renews. Human "downtime" is not like the "rest" of a car or a computer. In human downtime, the body is continually learning, especially when asleep.

The psalmist in the Old Testament attests to this: ". . . even at night my heart instructs me."—Psalm 16:7

Pang concludes that: "Even in today's 24/7, always-on world, we can learn how to blend work and rest together in ways that make us smarter, more creative, and happier." History's greatest figures highlighted in the various studies knew that their creativity and productivity were not the result of endless hours of toil. Their towering achievements resulted from modest working hours with plenty of breaks in between.

As a girl in my early teens, I was in a boarding house for a few years. Taking a one-hour nap (which we called *siesta*) after school each day was compulsory and enforced strictly by the school authorities. At the time, it made no sense whatsoever. My schoolmates and I were still full of great amounts of energy after school each day, so we did not see the need for what we deemed then as a redundant hour of naptime before continuing with our evening studies. We always wondered why the school was so strict about enforcing siesta time. But now I finally understand why. Nap time was enforced so we could rest and recharge before continuing with our evening studies.

Many countries also have a tradition of taking afternoon naps. Such naps are common in some Mediterranean, Latin

American, and Asian countries, such as Spain, Greece, Mexico, Brazil, and China.

You do not have to run yourself to the point of where you feel completely drained, tired, or even sick before you realize that you should take a break and recharge. The truth of the matter is this: "You cannot pour out of an empty vessel." In other words, you cannot be of any good to others when you are exhausted, rest/sleep deprived, and drained. Prioritize rest by incorporating it into your daily routine. Take the time to recuperate so you can recharge and be refueled as you go about your daily business.

Many of us wear different hats: We are wives, husbands, parents, caregivers, board members, supervisors, teachers, soccer coaches, community activists, volunteers—and the list goes on and on.

These roles are important. To add the greatest value to them, be sure to do something daily to recharge. My habit is to recharge during my quiet alone time. I pray, meditate, and just spend time resting. I am very intentional about this. I have practiced listening to my body for a very long time and know when I am close to running on empty. I never let it get too close to empty.

Even if it is just thirty minutes of quiet time that I am able to squeeze in daily, I use that thirty minutes well. That quiet time is not spent scrolling through social media or watching TV. Rather, it is thirty minutes of journaling, going for a walk to enjoy nature, simply resting, and taking a nap if needed. More importantly, it is thirty minutes of alone time. Irrespective of how busy you are, you can take thirty minutes to recharge. Lock yourself in the bathroom for thirty minutes if that is all you can muster.

I met Mila through a mutual friend. Mila is a very successful C-suite senior executive. She excels at her very demanding job. In addition to being a senior executive at the organization where she works, she is also a very active community member.

She volunteers in various capacities and attends all of her kids' sports games whenever she is not traveling for work. Mila is that mom who does it all. As you can already tell, she is an extremely busy individual.

But Mila was also exhausted mentally and physically. This was what she said to me in our very first session: "I love my job and all that I get to do. I have been truly blessed. But I feel as though there is never enough time in the day to accomplish all that I need to do. I feel this way every single day."

Mila worked late almost daily and did not go to sleep until the wee hours of the morning, only to wake up just a few hours later. And at the time of our first session, she had not gone on a real vacation with her family in a very long time because she had not had the time. Work and her other commitments did not permit her to. She was just so busy!

I told Mila that she had to find a way to incorporate rest into her daily routine, otherwise she would sooner than later crash and burn. Her primary physician had even told her that her stress levels were starting to impact her health, but she did not take the warning too seriously. "I'm fine" is what she would say to me during our sessions.

Mila and I started out with some basic adjustments to her life. We worked on creating boundaries around work. We also were able to set aside Sundays as her "rest day," a day dedicated to spending time with family and recharging before the new workweek began.

It took a while to make the needed adjustments, as Mila was so accustomed to being a workhorse and a busy bee. She complained about feeling guilty whenever she took time to rest by going for her daily thirty-minute walk in Manhattan to clear her mind on work days. But as she began to appreciate the value of rest, she eventually came to look forward to her rejuvenating daily walks. Getting outdoors and exercising her body helped to clear her mind and, much to her surprise, helped her to come up with solutions to the never-ending work issues she had to deal with daily.

She had to reluctantly let go of two of her volunteer activities because she was stretched far too thin and was struggling to fully commit to all that she had signed up for.

Mila also took the time to plan an all-inclusive summer vacation with her family for the first time last summer. When she returned, she exclaimed that she loved every moment and has now committed to planning two big family trips annually. She also plans on getting away on smaller trips as often as possible.

Forcing Mila to incorporate rest into her schedule helped her to rediscover herself and her joy in spending time with her family, and to intentionally create time for the things in life that she enjoys other than work.

As expected, she said that her colleagues have noticed the difference. She is not as tense and edgy as she used to be, due to her lack of rest and living an overworked lifestyle. She is now more relaxed and easier to work with as a person. In one of our most recent sessions, Mila mentioned that she will be going on an all-girls trip with a few of her closest friends, something she had never done before because she just did not think she had the time and she never gave much thought to such trips prior.

Mila is a totally different person now. She has promised to live a well-rested life going forward.

Rest can help us to achieve excellence in our work by allowing us to focus on our most important and challenging tasks. It stimulates problem-solving and creativity while also helping us to improve our learning. Rest is not only necessary for life and survival, it is essential for anyone who wants to achieve excellence in life.

KEY POINTS

◎ Rest can take many forms, such as sleep, naps, walks, meditation, hobbies, and vacations.

◎ Rest is not a passive or unproductive activity, but rather a vital component of work and creativity.

◎ The creative achievements and productivity of some of the world's most influential figures resulted from working for only a few hours at a time and resting from work afterward.

◎ "Deliberate practice" is a term coined by psychologist Anders Ericsson to describe a type of focused and systematic training that aims to improve one's skills and performance in a specific domain.

◎ Human "downtime" is not like the "rest" of a car or a computer. In human downtime, the body is continually learning, especially when asleep.

◎ Even in today's 24/7, always-on world, we can learn how to blend work and rest together in ways that make us smarter, more creative, and happier.

◎ You cannot be effective in your different roles by running on empty.

TAKE ACTION

◎ Emulate the world's greatest. Consider adopting the system of deliberate practice. Practice or work in short, intense sessions of eighty to ninety minutes, separated by well-planned rest periods of fifteen to twenty minutes.

◎ Do your most creative work in the morning. Work for sixty-to ninety-minute intervals. Rest and recharge in-between your work sessions.

◎ Find a way to incorporate rest into your daily routine and lifestyle. This will help you to recharge your energy, consolidate your memories, and enhance your creativity.

◎ Ensure you are getting enough sleep daily. Sleeping for at least seven to eight hours per night is crucial for memory consolidation and brain health.

◎ Studies show that our level of creativity is enhanced when we rest and get enough sleep daily.

◎ To balance your mood and energy levels, engage in other activities that are enjoyable, relaxing, and stimulating, such as hobbies, socializing, meditation, or exercise.

AIM FOR PERFECTION IN YOUR PURSUIT OF EXCELLENCE

CONGRATULATIONS ON MAKING IT this far. You probably have a notebook filled with ideas on how to start to relentlessly pursue excellence in different areas of your life.

As a reminder, you only have this one life to live. There is no do-over! This is not a dress rehearsal! This is it! Irrespective of what your circumstances are, you owe it to yourself to make the most of your precious life. You owe it to yourself to do your best with the gift of this one life, irrespective of the hand you have been dealt.

Under no circumstances should you choose to become a mediocre version of yourself just so you can fit in with a certain crowd. Under no circumstances should you lower your standards of excellence to please others. Even if you did, you will still not succeed at pleasing everyone. So do yourself a favor and hold fast to your high standards of excellence.

By the very definition, to be human is to be imperfect. We all have our flaws and shortcomings—there is no exception. However, that should not stop or prevent us from pursuing excellence in every single area of our lives.

People of excellence may be viewed by some as perfectionists. The truth is, there is absolutely nothing wrong with being a perfectionist. Just keep in mind that perfection is ultimately unattainable because those trying to achieve perfection are themselves full of many imperfections. It is a paradox. However, that should never prevent or stop us from trying to attain perfection because when we aim for perfection, even when we do not attain it, we will at least end up with excellent results. It is this striving for perfection—not its actual attainment—that produces a life of excellence.

This certainly beats starting off with an attitude of mediocrity. That mindset is like admitting failure before one even begins. If we have a mindset of mediocrity, we will never see great things happen. We will also never fully realize our potential and will fall short of becoming people of excellence.

So aim for perfection, knowing fully well that it is unachievable, but knowing that you will end up with excellent results for your efforts. Hey, you just never know, you might also end up with perfect results every now and again!

In the words of Norman Vincent Peale, "Shoot for the stars and if you fail, you'll land on the moon."

We all are facing different circumstances in life, many of which are out of our control. Do not bother with trying to control or change that which you cannot control or change. Your job is to do your best, irrespective of those circumstances. Get up each morning and give each day your best effort.

Be the best at your work.

Hone your craft and skill set.

Be an avid learner; that is how you grow and expand your capability and capacity.

Prove that you are capable of properly managing the resources at your disposal by making wise choices when it comes to how you utilize those resources.

By doing so, you are letting the world know that you can be trusted with more and eventually more will be offered to you. Remember always that you are a masterpiece, God's very own masterpiece.

My hope is that the principles of excellence outlined in this book equip you with the blueprint that you need to pursue excellence as an imperfect being living in an imperfect world.

My desire is that by putting these principles into practice, you get to experience the joy in each day and the beauty in each season, irrespective of your current circumstances.

I pray that you remember to give yourself grace when you miss the mark, and to try again when you fail at something, and to accord grace to others often.

Your relentless pursuit of excellence can coexist perfectly with the many imperfections within and around you. It requires effort, but I urge you to keep up the good work of relentlessly pursuing excellence in every area of your life. Make excellence an integral part of your identity, of who you are as a person. I am rooting for you!

ABOUT ADEYINKA ADEGBENLE

Adeyinka Adegbenle is an excellence strategist, coach, published author, and teacher. A former financial services professional, Adeyinka has a record of success in complex organizations that include Fortune 500 multinationals with 75,000+ employees and $30+ billion in revenue.

Through her coaching programs and courses, she has helped many obtain outstanding, measurable results by teaching and equipping them with dynamic processes, systems, and habits of excellence.

Adeyinka is the author of the highly acclaimed book *Joab, King David's Top General: Essential Lessons on Character Development,* and her latest book, *Master Excellence: 13 Principles to Help You Win at Life.* She also hosts and facilitates leadership workshops and seminars where she teaches leaders about excellence principles and systems that will help them excel in their roles.

She is the host of the Ways of Excellence Podcast on Youtube.

Adeyinka has also shared her stories with hundreds of thousands of listeners on many leading podcasts, including:

- *The Clever Girl Finance podcast with Bola Sokunbi*
- *The Business with Purpose podcast with Molly Stillman*

- *The CHARGE podcast with Gary Wilbers*
- *The Master Your Mind, Business. and Life podcast with Lauren Smith*

Adeyinka is a graduate of Long Island University, New York, with an MBA in international business relations. She holds a bachelor's degree from the University of Nottingham, United Kingdom. She is a Certified Project Manager (PMI-PMP), and she holds advanced certifications in teaching English to adults and young learners (TEFL, TEYL).

Adeyinka is also a wife and mother. She is an avid house plant lover and enjoys hiking and trying out different baking and cooking recipes.

ACKNOWLEDGMENTS

One of the major tenets of excellence is this: Excellence attracts excellence. From experience, I can say without a doubt that as I have grown and continued to pursue excellence in all facets of my life, I have attracted like-minded individuals who have been instrumental in helping me to get this message of excellence to the world.

One such individual is Kent Sorsky. I thank him for doing an incredible job with the editing of this book. In my search for an editor, I prayed a simple prayer: "Let my editor be one who has an eye for excellence." Kent, you do! Not only are you immensely talented at your craft, you do it with such a great attitude too. I am happy and proud of what we have accomplished. I hope we get to work together on many more projects in the near future.

I'm so grateful to my immediate and extended family members far and near. I have been blessed with wonderful parents, relatives, and inlaws. It has been said that "Being a family means you are a part of something very wonderful. It means you will love and be loved for the rest of your life." I do not take the assurance of the steadfast love that I receive daily from my family lightly. It acts as fuel to keep me going daily.

I am thankful for my church family. You are amazing through and through. I am so very fortunate to be part of a family of such loving people. You epitomize God's love and are such a delight to be with weekly. I find strength and hope in being a part of our family circle._

I also want to thank the many clients I have worked with over the years. Each coaching session leaves me with a deeper appreciation and belief in my work in this field. It never ceases to amaze me that I get to witness my clients transform into epitomes of excellence all the time. I get so much joy from helping each one of you grow, discover, and walk in your greatness. You have all inspired me in many more ways than you know.

I am grateful to my newsletter subscribers, followers on social media, and everyone who watches my weekly videos on YouTube. I love our community of excellence-minded individuals. Thank you for supporting my work over the years.

To my biggest cheerleader—my husband, Wale—thank you for believing in me even more than I believe in myself. Your steadfast encouragement, your love, and your support of my work means the world to me. The core values that you live by daily are truly worthy of emulation. You are an amazing human!

To Caleb, Chloe, and Isaiah, I am incredibly proud of all of you. I love watching you grow in excellence, wisdom, and understanding. I am immensely grateful that God saw it fit to make me your mom.

Last but not least, to Him who created us all to show forth his magnificent excellencies, I owe God my utmost appreciation. The Lord has always been so very kind and gracious to me. For that I am most grateful.

INFORMATION PAGE

I look forward to hearing from you and about your excellence development journey after reading this book. Tell me your story! I would love to hear how the excellence principles taught in this book have made your life better. Reach out to me directly at **yinka@yinkaadegbenle.com**.

Learn more about me and my work at **www.yinkaadegbenle.com**.

Join hundreds of other excellence-minded individuals for weekly messages on excellence strategies, processes, and general wisdom on how to win at life by signing up for my weekly newsletter: **www.yinkaadegbenle.com/newsletter**

For permission requests and inquiries, email: **contact@ yinkaadegbenle.com**

Connect with me on social media; let's share ideas on excellence in cyber space here:

Youtube: @waysofexcellence
X: @yinkasho

TikTok: @waysofexcellence
Instagram: @waysofexcellence
Facebook: @waysofexcellence

The Master Excellence Online Course

Do you want to dig even deeper into the practice of Excellence? The Master Excellence Course has been designed to let you learn about the 13 Principles of Excellence in lecture form and at your own pace. It is a great complement to this book. There are 10 modules in all. Each module covers a specific principle of excellence in depth. At the end of each module, you will be able to complete several questions designed to help you apply the principle you just learned to your life. Learn more and register for the Master Excellence Course here:

https://adeyinka-adegbenle-s-school.teachable.com/p/the-benefits-of-pursuing-excellence-in-everyday-living

ENDNOTES

1. "First things first: Family activities and routines, time management and attention." 2016. *Journal of Applied Developmental Psychology*, https://www.sciencedirect.com/science/article/abs/pii/S0193397316301241.

2. R. A. Emmons, M. E. McCullough (2003). "Counting blessings versus burdens: An experimental investigation of gratitude and subjective well-being in daily life." *Journal of Personality and Social Psychology*, 84(2), 377-389. https://doi.org/10.1037/0022-3514.84.2.377.

3. Y. Joel Wong, Jesse Owen, Nicole T. Gabana, Joshua W. Brown, Sydney McInnis, Paul Toth & Lynn Gilman (2018). "Does gratitude writing improve the mental health of psychotherapy clients? Evidence from a randomized controlled trial." *Psychotherapy Research*, 28:2, 192-202, DOI: 10.1080/10503307.2016.1169332.

4. A.M. Wood, S. Joseph, J. Lloyd, & S. Atkins (2009). "Gratitude influences sleep through the mechanism of pre-sleep cognitions." *Journal of Psychosomatic Research*, 66(1), 43-48. https://doi.org/10.1016/j.jpsychores.2008.09.002.

5. E. L. Polak, & M. E. McCullough (2006). "Is gratitude an alternative to materialism?" *Journal of Happiness Studies*, 7(3), 343-360. https://doi.org/10.1007/s10902-005-3649-5.

6. David C. McClelland. April 19, 2007. "Papers of David McClelland, 1900–1998: an inventory." Harvard University Library Online Archival Search Information System (retrieved on November 28, 2007, from http://oasis.lib.harvard.edu/oasis/deliver/~hua04001).

7. https://www.researchgate.net/figure/Classification-of-6-Virtue s-and-24-Character-Strengths-Peterson-Seligman-2004-Virtue_ tbl1_7701091

8. S. Kyeong, J. Kim, D. Kim, et al. (2017). "Effects of gratitude meditation on neural network functional connectivity and brain-heart coupling." *Scientific Reports*, 7, 5058.

9. https://pubmed.ncbi.nlm.nih.gov/19846255.

10. Masaru Emoto. *The Hidden Messages in Water.* 2004. Beyond Words Publishing.

11. Caroline Leaf. "How to Tap Into the Nonconcious Mind to Unwire Trauma & Toxic Thinking Habits."

September 11, 2022. https://www.linkedin.com/pulse/how-ta p-nonconcious-mind-unwire-trauma-toxic-thinking-leaf.

12. Masaru Emoto and Noriko Hosoyamada. 2005. *The True Power of Water: Healing and Discovering Ourselves.* Atria.

13. Division of Sleep Medicine at Harvard Medical School. (2007). "Sleep and disease risk." Retrieved June 12, 2017, from https://sleep.hms.harvard.edu/education-training/public-education/ sleep-and-health-education-program/sleep-health-education-86.

14. P. Posadzki, D. Pieper, R. Bajpai, et al. "Exercise/physical activity and health outcomes: an overview of Cochrane systematic reviews." BMC Public Health 20, 1724 (2020). https://doi.org/10.1186/ s12889-020-09855-3.

15. Alex Soojung-Kim Pang. *Rest: Why You Get More Done When You Work Less.* 2018. Basic Books. See also Pang's article "Darwin Was a Slacker and You Should Be Too" (https://nautil.us/darwin-was-a-slacke r-and-you-should-be-too-236532/).

16. Robert McCrum. "The best of times to write." *The Guardian.* October 27, 2011.

17. K. A. Ericsson, R. T. Krampe, & C. Tesch-Römer (1993). "The role of deliberate practice in the acquisition of expert performance." *Psychological Review*, 100(3), 363. https://psycnet.apa.org/buy/1993-40718-00.

Made in the USA
Columbia, SC
23 April 2024

079587c0-f62c-46ce-addc-5c2b835b62bcR01